Safe Harbor

Also by Judy Shuler

Red & Blue: A Memoir of Two Alaskan Tour Guides
(With Hildegard Ratliff)

Alaska Travel Planning Guide: Help for the Independent Traveler

Safe Harbor

Stories of Enduring Friendship

Judy Shuler

Ouzel Press
Fredonia, New York

Copyright © 2020 Judy Shuler

All rights reserved.

ISBN-978-0-578-57988-7

Dedication

For all the friends who have graced and defined my life.

TABLE OF CONTENTS

INTRODUCTION xv

Lunch With Friends 2

Mary Alice & Me 10

Ruby Jo & Me 20

Cheryl & Me 30

Kathy & Me 43

Hildegard & Me 56

Friends for Life 68

    Rita & Kathy & Kathy 68

    Debbie & Marcy & Kim 72

    Ginny & Mary 74

Spanning Time and Distance 79

    Tina & Linda & Becky et al 79

    Jenean & Kim 84

    Mary Alice & Nancy 87

    Hildegard & Renate 89

    Anne & Deborah 93

Friendships Forged in the Workplace 98

    Mary & Doris 98

    Mary & Marilyn 99

    Kate & Tammie 100

Soulmates 103

    Haruna & Ryoko 103

Transcending Differences 108

    June & Florence 108

    Sandy & Michelle 110

    Michele & Marisa 113

    Khady & Me 115

Friendships Among Guys 119

    Al & Bill 119

    Emory & Steve & Ken & Gary & Chuck 121

    Dave & Joe 123

    Ed & Dean 126

    Fred & Lloyd 127

Men and Women as Friends 133

    Her Closest Friends Were Men 134

    Kathy & Brian 136

No Words Needed **139**

    Mary & the Nuns 139

Chance Encounters **142**

    Hildegard & Liz 142

    Mary & Rita 143

    Erin & Erin 144

    Hildegard & Robin & Me 145

    Jerry & Sandy & Martin 155

Friends Who Save Us **159**

    Mickey & Lori 159

    Judy & June 167

    Hildegard & Michi 171

    Jeff & Judy & Andrew & Janey 173

When Family and Friendship Circles Blend **179**

    Barbara & Lloyd & Carol & Bill 179

    Elsie & Richard & Delana & John 181

    Anne & Steve & Sylvia & Herkey 182

Unexpected Endings **186**

    Kaaren & Nancy & Me 186

    Sarah & Mary Ellen 189

Friends at My Fingertips **199**

    His Friends & Mine 199

Pets As Friends **212**

    Tucker Comes Home 212

    About Tyler 216

    And Now, Bentley 222

    Donner—An Unlikely Companion 224

    Jesse the Dog 227

Digital Friendship **233**

    Kellen & Friends 233

    Friendship Beyond Facebook 234

The Serious Side of Friendship **237**

    Health for Body and Psyche 237

    ABOUT THE AUTHOR 247

Acknowledgments

Thanks to members of the Write Now Writer's Group at Ahira Hall Memorial Library, Brocton, NY, who encouraged and critiqued this book through every stage, with special thanks to Michele Meleen.

Deep gratitude to all who shared their own stories of friendship for Safe Harbor.

INTRODUCTION

This book was conceived on the night road of loss, and took a turn on another such road five years later. The first sharpened my appreciation for the meaning of friendship, the second re-defined my understanding of the depth and breadth of friendship in our lives.

My early years within my family were nurturing and secure, so tranquil I grew up wanting to test myself, to see if I could navigate beyond the boundaries of their safety. I wanted to venture out, to see if I could make my way in a wider world. A world where I would have to create my own circle.

It is the job of youth to strive and stretch and grow. Because my family set me free, they gave me the foundation to strike out even as I knew they were still there, ever ready to welcome me back. And to their great credit, they did not try to impose their life on mine, hold on tight or dictate the direction of my journey. I stood on tiptoes to gaze beyond the flat fields of hay and oats and Holstein pastures in rural Wisconsin. Looking at the family home that gave me so much security, the people who made me feel accepted and loved, I made plans to move on.

The university that opened my first job likewise felt stifling. Once I had my undergraduate degree in journalism I knew my academic life was over. It was time to start my life. Too immature for serious dating, I also knew I didn't want any boyfriend to tie me to this place. Classmates were pairing up for life after school; not me. It would take leaving that safe place for me to grow up and find a life that fit me. A life with friends. People who would make me feel as comfortable as my family had, needing me as I needed them.

I was also done with roommates, even while treasuring my college roommates and wanting to stay in touch forever though it would eventually be clear they did not. How did someone too reserved for dating think she'd be able to just move away and live on her own? With her own apartment.

My first job was with the *St. Paul Pioneer Press-Dispatch*. I loved the pace of a newsroom, the way being a reporter opened doors to people and places unlike any other job I could imagine. But St. Paul, MN, was a family-centered tradition-bound community like the rural area where I grew up. Still somewhat shy when not bearing the mantle of reporter, I found it hard to build a social circle after the work day ended.

Two years later I followed an inner compass pointing north and landed a personnel job with the Federal Aviation Agency in far-off Anchorage, Alaska.

For someone introverted as I was, it surprises me more in retrospect than it did at the time. I must have been more driven than even I realized. With phone calls home typically costing $25, we communicated by letters which I tried to write once a week. I once wrote my parents telling them I was so grateful they let me go. "We felt it was your life to do what you wanted," my mother wrote back. Still it must have hurt. When my one-day husband traveled to Anchorage on a whim and then against all intentions accepted a job there, his father's response was "Well, you got as far away from home as you could, didn't you?"

Anchorage was a city of newcomers. Almost everyone had come from somewhere else. Many had no family nearby, others only immediate family—spouse and children. Through friends we wove a family of our own making. There was a palpable excitement about being in this remote, wild place that folks back home could not even imagine. New arrivals were routinely invited to the homes of people who'd been there only a little longer. It was unthinkable not to invite singles home for holiday meals. Soon I had more friends than in two years in St. Paul. In six months I thought "I am home."

What draws us to a particular place? What makes some places feel so right and some so uncomfortable? I do not know, but I know the chain of circumstances that took me to Alaska took me to a home I would passionately embrace for 45 years.

Yes, it was the mind-numbing natural beauty, the wildness so unlike the manicured landscape of the Midwest, the feeling that this place was so different and so special. And it was the people who would become fast friends. No barriers, no sense that family was all and there was no need for outsiders. We were all away from family and reached out to each other.

Here at last I began to grow up and find out who I was through friends.

Friends who would follow me through time zones and zip codes. Though I now live hundreds and thousands of miles from most of them, they show me that true friendship has no boundaries. They continue to fill my life.

Friendship is a sanctuary, a safe harbor, a place of refuge in the sun and shadows of daily life.

True friends bring out the best in each other, each making the other a better person. They wholeheartedly celebrate each other's successes. They respect their differences as well as their common vision. They do not demand anything of the other. They trust each other without reservation. One of the gifts of years is learning which friendships endure, transcending time and distance.

These are the stories of my friendships, and those of others. Some are light-hearted, some unexpected, some truly life-changing.

Chapter One

My friends have made the story of my life.
Helen Keller

Lunch With Friends

I like to imagine gathering together five friends who span decades and zip codes, friends who define my life.

Mary Alice, Ruby Jo, Cheryl, Kathy, Hildegard.

We met at different times and in different places. Mary Alice and I share history that pre-dates grade school in rural Wisconsin where we grew up. I forged bonds with all the others in Alaska. Now I live two states away from her and across continent from others.

After 45 years in Alaska I moved with my husband to his family home in Western New York. A few years later, still somewhat adrift in my new life 3,500 miles away, I began thinking about friends who've followed me through the decades though I could no longer see or touch them. Shared coffee and meals and travel adventures were mostly just memories. Yet we stayed close—phone, texts, emails, occasional visits—and continued to be a part of each other's lives.

Some never met others, and they never will. Others met each other briefly in passing or knew each other casually. Some have not seen others for several years. For most, the etched memories are of our younger selves, when we were navigating a more complicated labyrinth of work and family, of defining ourselves and our journey. That has settled and slowed.

We could gather for lunch in Seattle. It's as close to Alaska as you can get in the contiguous states. Flying between Alaska and family homes in Wisconsin and New York, I always felt that when I reached Seattle on the way back north I was already home. It would be the perfect place to bring us together. A place where we all have histories and memories, yet neutral ground as none live there today.

I'd plan lunch at Elliott's Oyster House on Pier 56 overlooking Elliott Bay. I'd like a table on the open deck, where our senses could absorb the symphony of the sea on a sunny day. But I'd also welcome a quintessential foggy misty day shrouded in mystery—my favorite kind of day when I lived in Southeast Alaska.

There'd be fresh flowers on the table, a low arrangement of wild flowers so we could talk over it. And a real wax candle, lit in honor of candlelight talks some of us shared in years past. The menu would be a nod to our northern ties: Dutch Harbor King Crab Legs, Alaskan Sockeye Salmon, Pacific Rockfish. One concession to my current life in Western New York—I'd persuade the proprietors to let me bring in Rufus Red from Liberty Winery to share. It has become my local addiction.

At one time blue and white vessels of the Alaska Marine Highway glided north from here on their way to ports in Southeast Alaska, before the southern terminus was moved north to Bellingham in 1989. All of us have ridden state ferries, traveling between island communities and those with no road access. It is one of the things I miss most. Now boat whistles of Washington State Ferries docking at Pier 52 and the strident calls of gulls would spur memories of our one-time home in the Far North. With the unmistakable briny smell of the sea comes a sense that the whole Pacific Rim is within grasp.

If I had never moved from the Midwest to Alaska I would not be the same person today. Much as we may think we float over our surroundings to be ourselves, we are invariably colored by them. When I was a child going to county fairs, one of the popular concessions was an open pan of water with paint in various hues dropped on the surface. The operator would gently stir the colors around, then swirl in objects like glass or ceramic vases to be colored. Each would have a unique marbled pattern that could never be replicated.

Our lives are like that, dipped and swirled until something quite different emerges.

My Alaska fostered strong women, in them I saw what I wanted to be. Independent take-no-prisoners personalities. Most didn't lose their individuality or take their sense of worth from their family even while being married and raising children. Even the most capable could be feminine in traditional ways when they chose. Most lived far from parents and siblings, as I now did, finding friends to fill gaps and share interests beyond their immediate family circle. There was no hard edge between family and friends; they blended into a single circle of equal standing. Many a young person through the years has set out from home to a life of choosing or seeking, of course. Often it involves going from smaller town to bigger city. But few will find the open arms of a frontier where traditions are not set in stone, people not yet formed into camps.

To survive and even thrive, a healthy ego is required. Indeed, a feeling of self-worth is necessary to build strong friendships. To be needy and dependent is not the stuff of true friendship among equals. Contrary to belief, perhaps, ego is not a bad thing. But the people who outwardly portray the biggest ego of all are beneath it the most insecure. No wonder ego has a bad rap.

Federal employment provided my ticket to Alaska, but I was ill-suited for its shelves of rule books. Not surprisingly, none of my relationships from that office survived my departure. Friends came, and stayed, from where my passions lie.

Without a streak of independence and defiance of what was popular (California was the trendy destination at the time) we would never have ended up in the same state, and never have met at all. My life would be far narrower, less colorful, less fulfilled.

To gather for my fantasy lunch I and my five friends would fly into Seattle-Tacoma International Airport from the north, south and east. I'd arrive first, meet each one at the airport, and call the shuttle service for the nearby Double Tree Hotel, where I'd reserved their rooms. They'd get the hotel's signature fresh warm chocolate chip cookie upon check-in. I'd instruct them to meet me in the lobby the following morning for a courtesy shuttle. A limo would be fun, but too pretentious.

We've all been in Seattle more than once, some of us many times. Mary Alice went to Seattle on a road trip with her parents while still in school. She'd fly in from Wisconsin where she still lives. I first drove to Seattle with my parents en route to my new home in Anchorage. We delivered my car to SeaLand, a barge company that would transport it to Alaska. Even with the Alaska Highway constructed through Canada during World War II, nearly all goods arriving or departing Alaska were moved via their container ships. Then I flew north while my parents flew back home to Wisconsin.

Cheryl grew up in Portland. She would have flown in from Tucson. Ruby Jo flew to Seattle as a stopover on her way moving to Anchorage from New Mexico. Once Ruby Jo and I spent a long weekend there hitting all the tourist highlights. Kathy lived and went to college there before moving to Anchorage. Now she lives in Juneau and could take a direct flight in just under two and one-half hours. Hildegard originally passed through Seattle on her first venture into Southeast Alaska. Now she'd be flying in from her home in Denver.

The shuttle van would take us directly from hotel to the Oyster House. On the ride over the ones who knew each other would start to talk. Hildegard and Kathy knew each other best, Ruby Jo and Cheryl had met only briefly and would scarcely remember each other. Mary Alice would know only me.

What do even I know of them? There is much that I don't know, their daily lives before we met or during long geographical separation.

Four cases of unrequited love. No, make it six. Who hasn't had one of those? Divorces. Jobs that didn't work out or were eliminated. Four who stared down life-threatening illness. Four among us widowed. One never married, one numerous times. This circle accounts for only nine children, pretty small for six women. Three of us raised no children. One bore four, one three, one two. Those who were mothers defined themselves, I think, as that and also in other ways: teacher, writer and more.

None of us, when we entered the restaurant, would create a hush or turn heads. Two of us might be considered tall, one quite short, others in the middle. None are fashion mavens, though I am probably the most interested in design in all forms. Most are on the fair side, two are decidedly brunette. We'd all be dressed casually. Ruby Jo, short in stature with dark short hair and dark eyes, favored coordinating polyester pants and top from Alfred Dunner. Cheryl wore shorts and sandals after moving to the desert from the Northwest. Mary Alice and Kathy might both wear jumpers, Kathy in a Bohemian style. Both seasoned world travelers, they know the comfort of travel in skirts. Hildegard would wear slacks and sweatshirt, in shades of blue.

As usual, I would probably be the most dressed up. I'd wear the mother-of-pearl bracelet from Hildegard, the carved antler bird necklace from Kathy, the sterling silver bracelet from Ruby Jo, a silk scarf direct from China from Cheryl. Somehow I'd pull all them together to highlight each gift, probably with high leather boots, black, inspired by Kathy's trip to Belgium, a Lands' End turtleneck as I virtually lived my entire Alaskan life in them, and a tweed riding skirt I'd imagined I'd wear in my retirement. Most of my gifts from Mary Alice were for the house and my other passion, interior decoration. Hand-crocheted doilies, a covered milk glass candy dish.

At the restaurant a bottle of wine would be reminiscent of many I'd shared with Ruby Jo and Hildegard over the years. Cheryl bought a bottle of Great Wall wine for our trip to China, to share on steps of the Great Wall at Simatai. The bottle serves as a base for my mother's crocheted tree every Christmas, the cork is still in my collection. Kathy would choose sweet herbal tea; she's seen enough of alcohol abuse as a junior high school counselor. Mary Alice is no teetotaler, but I don't know that she's a wine aficionado either. We've lived our adult lives apart—there's much I don't know about her grown-up self.

I'd let them find their own seats, curious about how they would arrange themselves. I'd set out magazines as kind of place cards—would they take that cue for where to sit? *Guideposts* for Ruby Jo. *National Geographic Traveler* for Cheryl, though it would apply equally to Mary Alice and Kathy. All world travelers. *PC World* for Mary Alice. *Southwest Art*, or any art magazine, for Kathy.

For Hildegard, I'm not quite sure. Because I worked with her I have spent more actual time with her than any other woman friend, and I find it hardest to define her. The people and things closest in the frame seem too complex to sort out into manageable pieces. They are like a kaleidoscope, myriad tiny colored pieces shaping and reshaping themselves into ever-changing patterns. I once thought of life as a tapestry, now it feels more like a kaleidoscope, without defined selvages, warp and woof, not constrained to a place on the wall to be frozen in time.

My job as host—help them find common ground to begin conversing with the person next to them.

Though Mary Alice traveled in Alaska twice, she is the only one who's never lived there. And Cheryl is probably the only one who didn't think Alaska the greatest place she'd ever lived. So a common bond already. Mary Alice wrote computer manuals, Cheryl wrote travel guidebooks. I could start there. Both were good at what they did, both had the moxie to know it.

"So what have you been up to lately?" with emphasis on the word *you*, Kathy would say in her soft voice. I've never heard another timbre. She'd listen to the answer, really listen, then offer approving words. She is the great encourager, coaxing everyone into their better selves. Ruby Jo would start with *remember when?* Totally sentimental, she treasured time with friends above all else. Hildegard would start talking to me—because we've shared the most face time there's no end to what we can discuss, including future writing projects. As wine is poured and salads eaten, the conversation will take on a life of its own.

Mary Alice and Kathy might begin comparing their life-long travels. Ruby Jo and Cheryl could share their mutual health challenges and their love of dogs.

Everyone would be on their best behavior; would they have liked each other enough to want to meet again? I once introduced two long-time friends to each other. Because I held them both so dear, I thought surely they would also bond. But it was not to be. Friendships take their own path. They cannot be predicted or arranged.

Would my luncheon guests appreciate my getting them together, or wonder *what was she thinking?*

Chapter Two

When the youth Bible study and business were finished and it was time for games (usually boy/girl games in the dark corners of the church), you and I always went home.

Mary Alice

Mary Alice & Me

Mary Alice is the longest term friend at my luncheon, a friendship nearly as old as I am.

She is the epitome of stalwart dependable Midwest stock. The middle of three girls, like me she grew up on a farm.

Mary Alice is sturdy in body and spirit, with a broad face and weight she struggled with. We both prevailed over youthful pressures to smoke and drink.

You were never left wondering what Mary Alice thought. It was out there for all to see, expressed clearly and directly. There have been a handful of people in my life that I treasure as personal discoveries, as hidden treasures. Crusty on the outside, marshmallow hearts within. Krispy Kreme. She is one of them.

She was not part of my gang of four in high school, all of whom disappeared from my life decades ago. How did we forge this bond that endured even with big spaces in the middle? It must go back to those very early years when I didn't even comprehend what it meant to have or be a friend, too young to look much beyond the boundaries of my own needs and satisfaction. Youth is mostly egocentric, though there are some notable exceptions. I don't think I was one of them.

It would take my personal loss to bring my thinking about friendship, hers and others, into sharp relief.

Mary Alice likely did not envision, when she backed out of her Winchester driveway and headed north to US Highway 45 on a three-hour solo road trip, that she would inspire a book.

The previous November my big brother began having stomach pains. Since we lived 850 miles apart, I knew only via greeting cards, email and occasional telephone calls that they persisted, undiagnosed, through winter and spring. Then in late May Gene called with his diagnosis. Pancreatic cancer, with six months to live. By then he'd nearly used up his six months.

Distraught beyond words, I flew to his side shortly after diagnosis, and again when the end was near. On the first day of summer 2011 he passed.

I had been on the constant verge of tears since his phone call. The morning of the funeral, at the Eagle River United Church of Christ, it took all my focus to maintain a wisp of composure. I stood in the back of the sanctuary with his widow prior to the service, greeting people I scarcely knew, when she unexpectedly walked in. Mary Alice was an anchor when I was adrift in loss. I was touched more than I can say. But only later, when I looked back, would her act of kindness on that June day leave me breathless. I began thinking of friendship and all it meant in my life.

Of such moments are our lives made and intertwined. Similarly, relationships have been rent apart by not showing up, or by a few hurtful words that once uttered become irretrievable.

Our story begins in the bucolic countryside amid the dairy farms of Central Wisconsin, surrounded by acreage and the never-ending chores of our parents.

Nevertheless her parents made a point of taking their girls on summer road trips, during the golden age of the open road. I remember feeling a twinge of envy at their travels and when they were among the first in the neighborhood to get a television set. She continued to travel throughout her life, but settled a few miles from the farm where she grew up.

I traveled 3,000 miles once as a young adult, and except for a few major trips, stayed firmly planted for 45 years.

Like me she was introduced to church at an early age. We first met in Sunday School at the First United Methodist Church in Neenah which our families faithfully attended. It was a stone Tudor building that seemed to my young eyes a veritable castle. Unlike me, she has continued to make the church a center of her life, now designing and updating her Grace Lutheran Church website, helping prepare spaghetti dinners, knitting prayer shawls. After meeting people of faiths other than Christian I could no longer see it as the only pathway.

First grade found us in separate one-room country schools.

One-room country schools, one room, one teacher, dotted the countryside. Each grade was called individually to the front of the room for lessons on the blackboard, while other students were expected to study quietly at their desks. We all had recess with swings, teeter totter and merry-go-round twice a day. Our restrooms were outhouses. A paper red and green traffic signal at the back of the room was turned to green when the outhouse was free, red when it was occupied. We were expected to await a nod of approval from the teacher before leaving our desk, flipping the signal it to red when we left the room, and back to green when we returned.

My county school was an easy walk from home along a blacktop country road, less than the length of two city blocks. While other children carried their lunches and ate together at school, I walked home for lunch—dinner in a farm home and the heaviest meal of the day—served promptly at noon.

I was the only first grader and star of my little universe, once proclaiming after I answered a question correctly, "I guess there isn't very much I don't know."

Everything changed when our districts were consolidated and I had four new classmates who would follow me all the way through high school. Our third grade class picture in the school yard is so etched in my memory that I recalled it vividly years after the last time I'd seen it. Her pig tails were braided, mine were straight. Both of us wore bias-cut plaid skirts. Her cardigan sweater was buttoned only at the top, mine top to bottom. Both of us looked down.

Mary Alice reminded me of a story I've long forgotten.

"Do you remember how each spring we would craft small paper boats and fancy sticks and float them through the culvert at the end of the school driveway?" she asked. Honestly I didn't recall.

"We got into trouble for 'playing in the road' and had to stay in for the next recess. Then after taking our punishment, we went back to the same activity the next time we went out. It was such fun!"

In our small class, her friendship is the only one that transcended school and lasted through adulthood for me.

Throughout school our lives wove in and out around each other. While we traveled in a different group of friends in high school we both embraced 4-H, an organization designed to teach country kids skills around the house and farm through head, heart, hands and health. There we learned to cook and sew and care for farm animals. We attended club meetings together, planned fair booths together, competed for ribbons at the county and state fair. We both got our first taste of public speaking when we wrote and presented demonstrations of some skill we had learned, a kind of show and tell.

When she got her driver's license, her parents bought a VW Bug.

"They were quite weary of hauling me everywhere, and I quickly claimed that orange Bug as mine," she remembers. "With that freedom, you and I went to the youth fellowship meetings at our church. We were the only members of that particular church from our school, so we stood out from the others. Many years later I became reacquainted with one of the gals who was in that fellowship group with us. She reminded me that when the youth Bible study and business were finished and it was time for games (usually boy/girl games in the dark corners of the church), you and I always went home."

What I remember most about her Bug was watching her write down mileage on a notepad in the glove compartment.

The Bug didn't get a gas gauge until 1962 and she was keeping track of when to refill the tank.

We were competitive scholastically and in extra-curricular activities. Because we were seen as more "serious" than classmates, we both ended up officers of clubs. We went to high school basketball games only on occasion. Neither of us was cheerleader material. She played in band, the piccolo and clarinet. I was too self-conscious to try, sure that I'd mess up the entire band by missing my cue or playing the wrong note.

Mary Alice was more athletic than I was, better in the compulsory physical education. Unlike me, she was not the last one chosen when team captains picked their team. She surely had more confidence, and didn't need to leave home turf, as I did, to find a way into adulthood. She was more of what was then called a tomboy, spending time outside and doing farm work while I stayed inside in my mother's world of homemaking.

She was in Future Teachers of America, foretelling her life as a teacher. I was in Future Homemakers and went on to major in home economics until journalism lured me away. On our high school yearbook, *The Magenta,* she was advertising editor, I was literary editor. We were both in forensics and the National Honor Society. When the grade points were averaged in our small high school—graduating class numbering 59—I was valedictorian, which we both wanted to be, and she was salutatorian. As if any of that mattered the day we left high school behind. I know I wanted to grow taller than she was, and I did. Fall found us in different colleges an hour apart.

"Will I see mountains?" I implored at a very young age. "Who knows what you will see in your lifetime," my mother always answered. As a school girl I must have learned how Wisconsinian glaciers flattened the farmland beneath our feet thousands of years earlier. But it was over a decade later, living among the mountains and still-active glaciers of Alaska, when I understood what a glacier is and does.

Those mountains would separate me from Mary Alice in years to come.

Eventually we both became writers. While I wrote for newspapers and magazines, she was at the forefront of computer software. She continued to teach through her adult life, business subjects, then computer programs. The latter would grant her further travels around the U.S. as she wrote manuals and gave demonstrations on WordPerfect, a word processing program. Unfortunately no one could stand up to Bill Gates' marketing skills and anything not bearing the Microsoft label struggles.

She was way ahead of me at grasping and using the emerging technologies that would change life as we know it. And she succeeded at what I always wanted but never achieved, a career that included travel.

By then I was deep into life in Alaska, and our contacts were not frequent. Still Mary Alice remained a constant, a steady tie to my home ground. I'd usually call her and visit for a few hours when I came home to see my family. For years after I married I'd come to her house alone, leading her to tease that my husband was a fabrication, not a real person. "Faceless Fred," she dubbed him until they finally met by chance at a local supper club. But there were always cards and notes at Christmas and birthdays. When my September birthday rolled around she would declare that I was now as old as her, until I could resume my younger status again at her January birthday.

Of all the people I know, hers is my favorite love story.

She already had a boyfriend in high school, while that would be years away for me. Our senior class play was *Our Town*. I played Mrs. Gibbs, her boyfriend was Mr. Gibbs. In the ritual of signing each other's class yearbook, her entry in mine was the longest. She reminisced about Sunday School and 4-H, made a light-hearted reference to the class play and how she had first dibs on my stage husband. We live close enough together to make new memories, she wrote.

But time for new memories ran out and distance would define our lives. After I'd already moved from our home area she married my Mr. Gibbs and had a son and daughter. The relationship was not destined to last, though she never said why and I didn't ask.

The seeds of her real romance had already been sewn while we were still in high school, but it would take years for them to take root. Her parents were among several families who hosted agricultural exchange students, young people from other countries who came here to attend high school and learn about our farming. Joachim (Achim), a young man from Germany with sandy hair, an endearing accent, slightly crooked smile and engaging personality came to live with her and her two sisters. I knew she shortly had a crush on him, but so did most of the girls who met him. And there was an age gap–he was a decade older which matters quite a lot when you're in high school.

When Achim and I attended the same university 100 miles from home, he had a car and I rode back and forth with him on weekends, along with Carol, my roommate and close high school friend. I always made sure Carol sat next to him in the front seat. She dropped out of college after the first year. Though unspoken, I suspect part of the reason was realizing that her feelings for him would not be returned. Everybody liked Achim, some quite lot.

After high school and college Achim returned to Germany for a bride, then brought her back to our home area where he worked for food processors and they started a family of daughters. But that relationship, too, was not destined to last.

Though I was too far away to see how it came about, at some point Mary Alice and Achim created the marriage that was meant to be.

While I was running a tour business in Juneau she came on a cruise with her parents and had spaghetti dinner at our house. Later, in 2005, she came to Southeast Alaska again, this time with Achim. He was already ill, more so than either of them realized. The following year, he was gone. "He was the better part of we," she wrote in talking about his passing.

I haven't seen her children since they were very young. But our friend and computer guru in Juneau moved briefly to Minneapolis, and ended up working with her son. Later she would share her home with her mother, who lived to 103. What genes she has to live up to.

So many little intersections of our lives. So many reminders of her in my home now in Western New York. Her hand-crocheted doilies on the dresser, which she brought as gifts on one of her trips to Alaska. The covered milk glass candy dish that she sent after I complained I couldn't find a covered dish. The mossy green prayer shawl crocheted by members of her church she gave me after my brother's funeral. The birthday cards, emails and now texts and phone calls inquiring about our well-being, or my surgeries or Fred's final illness.

Now we text each other, checking in when unsavory local weather makes national news, follow up after one of us has illness or surgery, sometimes just something that reminds one of the other. When I return to Wisconsin to visit family I try to see her as well. If we were mildly competitive as kids, there's no sign in our adult lives. We are supportive and solicitous of each other.

She continued on in music, where it would take my husband to bring music into my life and give it the important place it holds today. Mary Alice has kept in touch with other women from our high school class and now meets them monthly over coffee. She once emailed me a photo with five of them and their names—I could not match up four of them.

She edits a newsletter for the local historical society in the small town where she lives, continuing the writing we both share. I came late to teaching, first helping friends learn computer basics. Thinking I could perhaps teach after all, I found a volunteer niche tutoring students through Literacy Volunteers of Chautauqua County. For most, English is their second language. We are both teachers, after all.

She would be surprised at her seat at my fantasy lunch, with friends with whom I've spent much more time in my adult life. She is direct and to the point. I am what a friend in Anchorage once described as inscrutable. Though we differ, we share our German roots and Midwest values: family, honesty, hard work, independence.

We were separated by miles and years for marriages and divorce, her child-rearing, loss of our husbands, the little events of daily living. Yet I feel we are tightly bound.

If romantic love is a mystery, friendship is no less so.

What I learned from her:

Keep up.

Keep moving.

Follow your heart.

Family matters.

Stay in touch.

Seemingly small kindnesses can mean the world to someone else.

Chapter Three

We go back a long way, but what a wonderful journey!

Ruby Jo

Ruby Jo & Me

There's a lot of water under the bridge. It was Ruby Jo Bixler's favorite saying for all the ways our lives flowed together since we first met as new Alaskans, and all that has happened since.

Water defined our life on the Pacific Rim. It is at water's edge that life feels limitless. Years later we continued to acknowledge anniversaries of the dates we arrived in Anchorage. Hers was March 29, 1967, from Artesia, New Mexico. Mine was August 13, 1965, from St. Paul, Minnesota. Of the four Alaskan friends at my fantasy luncheon table, she is the one I met first.

Our lives quickly intertwined after meeting at the downtown First United Methodist Church, at a single adults group called *Methkeys*. "Meth" didn't have the same meaning then, or the group would surely have had another name.

As young singles we were discovering Alaska and ourselves, excited about living in the "Last Frontier." To Alaskans, everywhere else is "Outside."

Admittedly it wasn't perfect.

Television evening newscasts were flown in on tape from Seattle for viewing a day late, roads were still broken from the great Alaskan earthquake of 1964.

The dominant scrubby black spruce were basically ugly, not what we had envisioned. Weather comes from the dry interior land mass and it never smelled like the sea, even though it is built on the shores of Cook Inlet. Anchorage air is so dry it hurt my nose and tightened the skin on my face. Dust filled summer air after a few days without rain

But we embraced the beauty and vastness of the Alaskan landscape that defy description. Mountains surrounded us on three sides, with ocean waters on the fourth. Moose roamed freely through suburban neighborhoods, stepping over five-foot chain link dog fences with ease. Winter days sparkled with hoarfrost. It was all so different from the desert Southwest and the flat Midwest. Both of us forged a bond with the natural world we'd never had before. We looked around and saw daily miracles.

Together we drove to local campgrounds and parks, windows open wide, singing *I Love to Go a-Wandering* or *The Wayward Wind* at the top of our voices. Hers was better than mine, and earned her a place in the Anchorage Community Chorus, one of the quality musical groups in a city still rough around the edges. Visitors were and still are surprised at the richness of the arts in Alaska and her alto voice was part of it.

For Ruby Jo things like skiing, camping out by the creek, building a campfire and cooking a meal outdoors were all new. "But I began to unwind and I loved it," she said. "We nearly froze when we would go out in the early mornings and play tennis or go to the sunrise service on Easter. We were young, and it didn't bother us."

In early years our social lives revolved around the dozen or so members of our Methkey group. They included young airmen and soldiers from Anchorage's two large military bases as well as civilians. Anchorage readily embraced its military members—most didn't sense any separation between those rotating through and those of us staying on. One airman, tall and trim with a slight cleft lip, made it his side mission to also rotate through nearly every one of the girls in our group. He married one, though as it turned out only for a short time.

I was one of the few in the group to own a car, a turquoise Buick Special I brought to Alaska by barge. On Sunday afternoons after church we'd pile in my car for brunch or a picnic, or a drive down the Seward Highway. The highway along Cook Inlet is now a National Scenic Byway, but we didn't need a designation to know how special it was.

It was in Methkeys that I cast an eye on my future husband. After our first date and first kiss, I knew intuitively that Fred would be mine. Nevertheless, I named Ruby Jo my campaign manager. Together we drove past his apartment building looking for his powder blue Karmann Ghia. She gave me a simple sterling silver bracelet as symbol of her role, which I wear to this day.

She was my maid of honor of course, in a red velvet dress and muff I sewed for our January wedding. And she fancied the best man, still a bachelor, but it was not to be. She remained single.

After our marriage she continued to be a frequent guest in our home, part of the package. When Fred needed notes transcribed for a college-level course in banking she brought her legal secretary skills to bear and typed them for him.

On Halloween she dressed up and answered our door to trick or treaters with such verve it was hard to tell which side of the door was having more fun. When she had an evening paper route, she stopped at our house to warm up.

She was Auntie Rube to our two dachshund blends, Herman and Gus, house-sitting and dog-sitting when we left on vacations. They ran to the front window in total abandon whenever she approached. The mere mention of her name sent them into a frenzy of excitement.

Our travels together were not over. Ruby Jo and I flew to Seattle, just to play tourists. We took the elevator to the top of the Space Needle for lunch, looking down at the city as it rotated 500 feet above ground. We went to the storied waterfront Pike Place Market where fishmongers toss fish through the air and crafts and farm produce have equal footing. We toured Seattle Underground, a network of underground passages and basements that were at ground level when the city began in the mid-1800s. After the city burned in 1889 a new one was built above it. So much Alaska-bound commerce and travel passes through Seattle that it felt like home.

We drove to Mt. McKinley National Park for closer looks at the ice cream sundae-shaped Mt. McKinley that defines the vast wildness of Alaska. It's often visible from Anchorage and not a clear day passed when we did not ask "did you see the mountain?" Since then both the park and North America's highest peak have been returned to the original name *Denali*, the "Great One," bestowed by Athabascans who lived there for thousands of years. We took four-hour road trips to Homer, a little town at the head of Kachemak Bay in a setting so spectacular that everyone in Anchorage fantasized about how they could make a living there.

Then Fred was offered a job transfer to Juneau, a couple days away by road and ferry or an hour and one-half by jet. We broke the news to Ruby Jo over drinks at the downtown Captain Cook Hotel. She went home and cried. When we realized there would be no more shared lunches or bottles of wine, no more hanging out, it felt like we'd been ripped apart.

After 13 years I fully expected to live and die in Anchorage. It was not a move I embraced. Fred and I flew to Juneau for a week to look around and check out housing. There I found at last the lush tall spruce I had envisioned when I first moved to Anchorage, and like nearly everyone seeing it for the first time, was enchanted by the beauty of Southeast Alaska. Mountains surrounding the Anchorage bowl suddenly seemed distant compared to a city built right at their base and crawling up the sides.

We came home with a house under construction, and I began my internal transition of separating from a place I loved and where I had carved a place for myself. I do not remember the last time Ruby Jo and I were together in Anchorage, but surely it came with promises of visits in both directions. Juneau is a generation older than Anchorage, and it would take several years to feel the same connection that I found in Anchorage in six months. We kept in touch, as always, with Christmas and birthday gifts, cards and phone calls.

Telephone calls were more affordable by then. When we first came to Anchorage, a long distance call routinely cost $25.

After we'd moved to Juneau and I didn't see her regularly she had bouts of dizzy spells that doctors originally diagnosed as Meniere's Disease. But it was much more—tumors around the brain stem that required two lengthy surgeries and reconstructive surgery for partial paralysis they created on the right side of her face. She had to learn to chew again. Salads would prove most problematic. Later there would be colon cancer and enough abdominal surgeries that I suggested a zipper across her abdomen. People she'd befriended all those years stepped up to her side and through it all her positive attitude prevailed. I should have flown to her side, and I still regret that I didn't. I'm sorry. But Ruby Jo continued to be strong.

Eventually she came to Juneau for visits. We rode the Southeast Alaska Marine Highway ferries, drove mountain roads on a Golden Circle trip between Haines and Skagway via Yukon Territory. In Skagway we rode the narrow gauge White Pass & Yukon Route railway built for gold seekers in 1898. We walked to the grave of Soapy Smith, a notorious con artist and gangster. The ground was uneven and not easy for her to walk, but she was never one to hold back if she could help it.

By then we'd lost Herman and Gus. On another visit she met Tucker, a dachshund mix rescue dog we adopted from a shelter near our summer home in Western New York. Tucker never got the memo about how much Ruby Jo loves dogs, and to my great embarrassment completely ignored her for the entire week.

Fred was retired and had already gone back to New York for the summer, so it was just the two of us in Juneau. The Kentucky Derby was televised during her stay and we watched all the coverage, especially taken with the hats. Every year after, each of us would watch the derby in our own homes and call each other to discuss the hats and horses. A few years after moving to New York full time I decided seemingly out of the blue that Fred and I should host a Kentucky Derby party. Bodacious hats required. We'd serve mint juleps and Kentucky-inspired food. Guests could guess the winning horse and vote for their favorite hat. Everyone would take home a red rose, symbol of the Running for the Roses. Looking back, I think it was inspired by that derby weekend with Ruby Jo. After the race we'd discuss it by phone. I'd imagine her at my Derby parties too.

She was one of twins. Her mother died in childbirth along with her twin brother. Ruby Jo was so tiny she easily fit in the palm of her father's hand. So frail her mother's burial was held up to include her as well. Yet she survived.

When she was four she and her older brother got a stepmother who would raise her to adulthood. After college she was pronounced qualified to be a legal secretary, a profession that would take her through life. I believed she was capable of being more than a secretary but she never questioned it. Ruby Jo grew up, as many of us did, accepting pre-defined roles for women.

Feeling sheltered and overprotected by her very religious stepmother, she grew restless in the small oil towns of New Mexico. When a spirited high school classmate moved to Alaska and invited Ruby Jo to follow, she did.

Ruby Jo was eager to make friends and please other people, something that she would later realize caused her to lose herself. If someone needed a soft shoulder, she was there, encouraging them to talk. She dog sat and cat sat, she took the children of friends and co-workers to movies, bought them birthday and Christmas cards, spent every day and night in motion. She kept in touch with so many people that she was on the phone even when visiting us.

She became for many people a bridge over troubled waters, listening to their problems, their troubled relationships, their disappointments. Always juggling the needs and wants of others. Today she would be texting with smart phone in one hand, iPad in the other, simultaneously. People pulled at her hem wherever she was. Whenever someone wanted a favor or listening ear, she was there. Their lives became hers.

Friends with relationship problems turned to her for advice like going to a priest. Too often, she said later, she heeded opinions of friends rather than her own.

"Keep smiling" was her mantra, and her perpetual sunny disposition was a joy to be around. It is what drew people to her. Surely we all used her, took advantage of her willingness to help.

Gradually she made small turns from her upbringing. She left the Methodist Church in which she was raised to join the Episcopal Church. She broke the no-alcohol rule of her upbringing, as I did, to make wine a regular part of our outings, and later, enjoy a nightly bourbon. Raised a Republican, she became a Democrat. Taught to believe pre-marital sex was wrong, she nevertheless did not judge friends who did not agree. Though firm in her church, she did not believe those who do not attend are condemned. Over time she grew more spiritual than denominational, though you cannot understand her without understanding the role of religion in her life.

Slowly she began to re-claim her life, her me-time. To set her own pace, her own schedule. She no longer sought the approval of everyone, or listened when they deigned to tell her what she should do. Content to stay at home, she kept track of friends by phone, including several who no longer live in Alaska. Birthday and Christmas gifts always included a little toy for pets. She learned to say NO. And I said YES, it is your time.

Two beige pillows are propped on the white rattan love seat in my sun room in New York, gifts from her after I'd moved from Anchorage. One is embellished with roses and reads "I have a bouquet of friends but you are my rose." The other has flowers and leaves surrounding a red circle. Inside the circle it reads "Old Friends are the Best Friends." She often gave gifts with positive sayings about friendship and love. One ornament from her, with Winnie the Pooh silhouettes, says "Good Friends Will Follow You Anywhere."

A month before moving out of Alaska I flew north to Anchorage to visit her. Problems with balance and arthritis impeded her own ability to travel. Though we lived in separate cities for 32 years, we shared a common bond—we were both Alaskans with a capital "*A*." I sensed it would not feel the same when we lost that commonality. I also thought it might be the last time I would see her. But thankfully there would be at least two more times when I could plan layovers in Anchorage to see Ruby Jo after visiting friends in Juneau.

I live among vineyards and wineries now, something she would surely appreciate, remembering all the bottles we shared. Sometimes we chilled wine bottles in cold glacial streams on impromptu picnics. For it was in Alaska, probably with her, that I first began to appreciate wine. If she could have traveled here I would have taken her to some of the nearby wineries.

We spoke by phone and texted as easily and naturally as though we'd lived in the same city all these years. True friendship does not end when we dwell apart. We talked about our weather, so often polar opposites. She inexplicably supported the Buffalo Bills. We gave a nod to the Iditarod Sled Dog Race and Fur Rendezvous, Anchorage institutions. No call was complete without lengthy discussion of politics and current events and her hearty laugh.

"We go back a long way, but what a wonderful journey!" she wrote in response to my letter to her. "We have been through a lot together, and we will continue to share with each other. Although we live apart now, distance does not sever love. It's as if you are next door when we talk on the phone."

On birthdays and at Christmas we'd look forward to each other's packages, typically including something good to eat. And always a toy for my dog.

For my September birthday she sent a large dark chocolate bar with dried blueberries that I ate in a single day, a candle in a pottery vase with a wooden lid, a gift certificate for Applebee's. She fretted the rubber squeak toy shaped like a taco might be too big for Bentley. I assured her it was fine, as he squeaked away during our phone call. As usual we discussed politics, in Alaska and the nation. Ten days later, without warning, she passed in her sleep.

Like me, she felt she grew up in Alaska. Anchorage is embedded in her soul. A friend gave her a plot and she is buried there as well. My ashes are to be cast in the waters of Southeast Alaska, so it is unlikely our remains will meet. But surely our spirits will.

What I've learned from her:

Other people matter.

A sunny spirit will take you far.

You can decide to be happy.

Sometimes you have to do what's right for you.

Chapter Four

Look at how the people are always singing.
Cheryl

Cheryl & Me

It's complicated.

That's Cheryl Probst-Teal. Born of the wayward winds, she was a product of the Pacific Northwest, scene of her early wanderings. Largely estranged from her family, she didn't talk about them much though a stepmother was involved. A sister who writes bodice rippers edging on porn stopped talking to Cheryl for unknown reasons.

Cheryl both knew who she was and fought harder to find herself than anyone I know. She grew up in Portland, graduated from Linfield College, worked as reporter for a small daily in Oregon, and was subsequently hired as staff writer by the Anchorage Times in Alaska. When we met in the Times newsroom in the early 1970s she was a reporter and copy desk editor and I wrote features for what was then called the women's page. As political reporter she was on first-name basis with the movers and shakers in a new state. The journey of her life is likely not one she could have imagined at that time.

More than seemingly so today, blunt directness was a hallmark of journalism. Janet, a fellow reporter and mutual friend, berated a public relations man who had lied to her with such ferocity that she literally reduced him to wordless jelly. It was that same kind of fierce independence that would carry Cheryl far beyond me.

We left Anchorage at about the same time. I moved to Juneau, Cheryl moved to Washington State. A few years later she bought a weekly newspaper, the Franklin County Graphic, in Connell. She hired Janet, who also hailed from the Northwest. We were all pleased for them. But Cheryl learned what many others have. Hiring friends can be dangerous, especially when both are independent and headstrong. The friendship and the job both ended. Sadly, so did Janet's life, with the devastating Lou Gehrig's disease.

On an agricultural exchange trip with a group of other writers Cheryl found her true home of heart. China. The China that Cheryl discovered was quite different from China today. Nixon had opened relationships between the two countries just a dozen years earlier. It was far less westernized. Wal-Mart had not yet caused Made in China to be both revered and despised.

Cheryl was smitten.

Owning her own weekly was a struggle; she moved on to other work. She looked for ways to return to China, and a decade later landed a job as editor for the English-written China Daily. The newspaper brought in English-speaking journalists to edit stories written by Chinese reporters and correct grammar and context for an English-speaking audience. Each contract was for a year; she managed to sign up for two.

When she moved to China she trusted me to handle her finances at home. Did I neglect to tell her I never balanced my checkbook before I married an accountant? Thankfully, she said she'd quit balancing a checkbook decades ago after spending eight hours trying to find a $2 mistake. And I did a good enough job with her finances that she still had money when she got home.

We said that if she went to China, we'd visit.

She meticulously planned an insider's view of China, and we landed in Beijing in 1995 on the cusp of major changes. Private citizens had just been given the right to own autos. They had yet to grasp the concepts of traffic lanes and signals that change from green to red. Traffic lights were routinely ignored, traffic lanes did not exist, cars and buses were both driven without lights at night. And they did not slow down for anyone for any reason. Cars passed frighteningly close to pedestrians, bikes and other vehicles at full speed. They passed anywhere, anytime, and if a car happened to be coming from the other direction, a two-lane road simply became a three-lane one.

The streets of Beijing remained one of our strongest images. Wide boulevards and narrow roadways, all filled with people and brand new drivers. Pedestrians, bicycle riders, street vendors selling everything from fruit to silk clothing to fried rolls.

Crossing an intersection was the third scariest thing we did on our visit. The second was riding in a car for hire, coming within inches of children playing on the roadside and bicycles loaded with everything from baskets to sofas, as the driver created his own passing lane as needed.

The first scariest was the subway, which Cheryl wanted us to experience as a local.

She assured us we would miss rush hour traffic. Unlike our public transport which limits numbers for safety, Chinese say there is always room for one more. A heart-warming philosophy until you see it in action. People crowd on at the same time others are trying to get off, and if you don't stand your ground near the door on board, there's no way you'll ever get off at your stop. By the time Fred could push his way off, he was pulled half-way out of his jacket. What was frightening was not the prospect of falling victim to a pickpocket, but simply getting on and off while the subway train remained stopped. With simultaneous ingress and egress of so many people at once, I imagined my feet might lift off the ground, be carried forward and abruptly set down again. Or not set down. Once on board, I felt I might never be able to get off again. And what if we were separated? How would we ever find each other amid Beijing's 12 million people? I could imagine spending an entire lifetime on the subway without ever being able to reach the exit door. We said no more subways. NO MORE SUBWAYS.

It was early March, chilly but not cold. She showed us kite-fliers in the parks and put a yellow dragonfly kite in our welcome-to-China kit, along with the famous sandpaper toilet paper. She drew our attention to groups exercising and performing tai chi in public parks. We went to an open air market where eels and all variety of flesh hung in the open, already attracting flies. We ate street vendor rolls that were cooked over a stove made from coals in an oil drum, veal on a wooden skewer, and dough that was rolled out very thin, spread with beaten egg and spicy sauce, fried and then folded around a crunchy sheet that reminded me of Rice Krispies. She thoughtfully spared us restaurants where you can pick out a live snake in a tank to be skinned and cooked at the table (she swore she once heard them screaming), and restaurants where menus can include what we think of as pets. I was also firm that I would not eat any skewers of little birds.

"Look at how the people are always singing," she pointed out with such affection for this place that captured her heart. Cheryl loved the color and festivity of Chinese New Year. She loved the hutongs, narrow streets or alleys that sold silks. My box of scarves, one of my favorite accessories, includes large silk squares from China. Not from China via Macy's but from hutongs, carried home in her luggage. In beautiful bold florals that could hang on my wall as well as around my neck.

The Forbidden City, Summer Palace, Lama Temple were all on our whirlwind itinerary. She took us to Mass in a cathedral which dated back two centuries and was re-built after destruction. A window had been broken and sparrows soared high above at the cathedral peak, their chirping filling the sanctuary with a universal language. Though not a practicing Catholic, Mass in Beijing's few Catholic churches seemed to speak to her.

She took me to the home of a woman who taught her how to roll dough and fill dim sum, or Chinese dumplings, so I could learn as well. Her teacher gave me the small rolling pin to take home. I still have the cork from Great Wall wine we sipped at the Simatai section. Amazingly, we were almost the only people there, a rare gift in such a heavily visited attraction. At the base on the way back I was introduced to my first pit toilet, as unkempt as I'd expected it to be, but not as totally off-putting as I thought.

Her friends in China included an English writer who ran the entire Great Wall and a Chinese family she remained in touch with.

After returning from her second year-long stint with China Daily she transitioned back to life in the United States by staying in our New York house and working briefly for a newspaper there. But her American heart was in the Northwest, and soon she was on the road headed west, in a car so questionable I asked her to call daily, pre-cell phone era, to make sure she was okay. She was.

Back home, another phase of her life awaited. A 21st century romance that began on the internet.

"I was just looking for great sex," she joked. What followed was so much more.

She married Jon in her 50s, an age when she could assure the officiating clergy that family counseling need not include forthcoming babies. Cheryl spoke in a slightly high-pitched voice that went up at the end of sentences. With her short blonde hair, a round face and rounded shoulders, she and Jon looked very much alike, something I was not the only one to notice. After her wedding in Washington State co-workers wondered aloud if she'd had a personality transplant. Gone was the brusque blunt Cheryl who could set aback friends with outspoken comments. In its place, a kinder gentler Cheryl who had found peace that seemed out of reach for so long. Marriage was transformative. She had a family at last.

I visited her and Jon at their home not so long after. As she had in China, she went to great lengths to introduce me to her home area. We went to Maryhill Museum of Art with peacocks on the lawn, the Columbia River Gorge below and an unexpected permanent collection of sculpture of Auguste Rodin.

Shortly life would shatter her newfound contentment. Jon was at work, riding a motorcycle he was repairing across a parking lot when he struck concrete and sailed off. He was not wearing a helmet and suffered a concussion. Her anguish was boundless, her support unwavering.

Eventually they bought a travel trailer which Jon proceeded to fix up, and sold their house in Kennewick. They planned to travel the United States for a few years, working as camp ground managers to finance their lifestyle. Cheryl had already written travel guidebooks about China. Now she would continue to write about the destinations and attractions they found along the way and publish them online. It was December by the time they closed on their house and headed south toward the Desert Southwest. Riding down the road it hit her: "I don't have a home anymore." What initially seemed freeing suddenly felt rootless.

Cheryl was diabetic. One of its side effects is sores that do not easily heal. For years she walked and rode bicycle to counteract diabetes, especially when she knew her diet had strayed. She was treated for a sore on her toe before leaving Washington and pronounced healed. Barely into their trip south, she realized that clearly she was not.

She ended up at a top wound care clinic in Yuma, AZ, for ongoing treatments and was told at varying times she would lose a toe or foot to amputation. Being stuck in one trailer park over a year was not the retirement on the road they had envisioned. This time it was Jon who was caregiver, daily cleaning and bandaging wounds. She insisted there would be no amputation but bits and pieces of her toe were removed.

Jon cared for her wounds even as he grew bored and restless. He started looking at houses everywhere. They wanted a house as base, with RV to travel in off-months.

An open wound on her butt sent her to a hospital again, with more care-giving from her husband. Her energy sapped by the heat and a daily routine of medical appointments that left little time for anything else, she set aside the writing that she so doggedly pursued. She called me frequently and I could sense the fear and frustration she must be feeling.

Sometimes listening is the best we can offer. I might have made a good psychiatrist, she told me once. "I have burdened you with my problems many times, but still you listened to more. I always feel more optimistic after talking with you. Having a friend who will listen like that is like having a MasterCard with no limits–it's priceless!"

Finally she was discharged and they headed back to Washington State where they still had belongings stored and family ends to tie up. Once again the wound on her toe festered and they had to spend money they had saved for a house on healing.

Torn about where they would settle, Jon thought about his late parents' house in Washington. She said "absolutely not!" and they headed back to the Southwest that they had grown to appreciate despite her need for constant care there. It was away from the cold weather she wanted to escape all her life, with open trails for motorcycle riding that was a focus of his. They wanted to live near Tucson, unfortunately so did everyone else. The cost of housing drove them to look about a 45-minute drive away. Cheryl wanted to be close to public transportation as she no longer drove, he wanted a garage big enough to work on his motorcycles. They made an offer on a house with a garage, in a small town away from bus lines.

She had one of the most challenging lives I know. I could not for a week survive the uncertainties of her life. She talked about her difficulties, how she gets hysterical and cries, yet she always came around to a positive note. Talented, inventive, determined, she had an imagination for her writing projects that far exceeds mine, and saw them through to completion.

Through most of her life, with a few interruptions, she kept up freelance writing. Cheryl saw opportunities everywhere she went and in everything she saw. She wrote guidebooks for travel to and within China and for places to visit in the Pacific Northwest and Desert Southwest. She wrote podcasts before I even knew what they were.

She continued to write even from RV campgrounds with limited or unaffordable internet connection. Somehow she found a way to make it work. She stepped into the world of online and self-publishing when it was still foreign to many of us. Her resourcefulness in finding outlets online for her freelance writing never failed to impress me. She generously edited work for me, and I read and made suggestions for her work.

Like most writers and photographers she failed to get the monetary rewards her work deserved. If her imagination and hard work were truly compensated, she could have purchased a house and garage in the heart of Tucson.

Her one surprising hold-out, she would not text.

Cheryl had other jobs along the way, as I have, but likely we both thought of ourselves first as writers. The women she kept in touch with are writers, most hearkening back to her days in an Anchorage newsroom.

The day I returned home from the hospital with a new knee I found a small package from our mail carrier on the front porch. Inside were paper butterflies with little magnets to alight on a refrigerator, a good-luck symbol from China. And mother of pearl necklace and tea, both of which she brought directly from China. She sent fresh olives and olive oil from a California processor they visited. Walnuts from a farmer's market. Tangerines from a tree in their trailer park. Fresh pecans and authentic salsa followed by an email warning–HOT! Hand-made laminated calendars with her photos. We shared a love of photography, and her images reflect an artist's eye with patterns in color, light and shadow that transform everyday objects into calendar-worthy photos.

When my husband passed she asked the time and date of his memorial service so she and Jon could think of him and observe a time of silence although he and Jon had never met. Suddenly left alone and struck by the uncertainty of time my priorities quickly re-aligned. Seeing friends I hadn't seen in several years, including her and Jon, floated to the top.

That spring they were my second stop on a trip to reconnect in person. Little did I know our visit would be filled with art and inspiration and natural wonders. It was a much-needed diversion in my altered state. From their home out of San Manuel, Jon drove 1,000 miles sharing their favorite highlights.

On the first day I checked off my bucket list a place I never thought I'd see, Frank Lloyd Wright's Taliesin West. I've been a FLW groupie for decades, taking friends several times to Graycliff near my New York home, visiting Falling Water in Pennsylvania, his home and studio in Oak Park, IL, and Taliesin East, his summer home and school near my alma mater in Wisconsin. Though not as familiar with Wright, they were as taken as I was with his winter home and school.

The next day—every day brought something new—I was inspired by an artist I'd never heard of. We traveled to the art studio of the late Ted DeGrazia who painted Native Americans around him. Like FLW, he was grounded in and by his surroundings. Like Wright, no detail was too small for his attention. He designed the studio that displays his paintings, pottery and bronze; his nearby home; and a small chapel. His gardens and courtyard are filled with whimsical art, he was as versatile in his own way as Wright.

Those two days inspired me to live with more intention, more style and artistry. To be more excited and purposeful about my life. Grace, not fear.

There would be more to see, of course. The centuries-old Casa Grande Ruins National Monument, with a Great House that was one of the largest prehistoric structures built in North America. Sonoran Desert People mysteriously abandoned it six centuries ago, along with wide-scale irrigation farming and extensive trade connections which lasted over a thousand years. We saw a pair of great horned owls raising four young there.

Another day, another road trip. St. Anthony's Greek Monastery, a favorite of hers, was wrested from the desert in just 20 years. What an unexpected contrast, with parquet floors, crystal chandeliers, intricate carved chairs and lecterns, citrus and olive trees and icons imported from Greece. My mid-calf skirt, which shrank an inch in washing, barely passed their strict visitor dress code requiring covered head, arms and legs.

My reminds-me-of-Alaska moment came when Jon drove us to the 8,000-foot level of 9,159 foot Mt. Lemmon. It was sunny when we left their house, overcast when we left the Tucson Wal-Mart, misting and blowing with a hint of snow by the time we got to 8,000 feet. Definitely like Alaska. Our picnic turned into sandwiches in the car and my fastest dash ever to an outhouse.

For locals it's an escape from summer heat and an unexpected winter playground with ski lift. Among founders of the ski club were Lowell Thomas and his son Lowell Thomas Jr. The latter was lieutenant governor of Alaska and attended church with Ruby Jo.

The paved 27-mile Mt. Lemmon Highway has been designated a Scenic Byway, just like the Seward Highway out of Anchorage. It begins in vegetation of Lower Sonoran desert and climbs to the high forests that reminded Cheryl of the Pacific Northwest and me of Alaska.

Cheryl was a Facebook fiend chronicling our every tour online. My best purchase for this trip was spare hair to cover the dry, stick-straight real thing beneath. The second best, a tablet to keep up with email and news, as they did not have television.

I am moved whenever I am welcomed into the homes and lives of friends. Just as I take something away from them, I know I will leave something of myself behind. The highest compliment from hosts is when they don't want you to leave.

Cheryl's battle with diabetes-related infection continued after my trip. A few years later she sent an email.

"Hope your Thanksgiving was better than ours. I overcooked the turkey and the pumpkin pie, the dressing was soggy, the gravy runny, the cranberry Jell-O salad didn't set. The only thing that came out OK was the olives, but if I'd had to do anything more than open the can, who knows!

"And I so wanted this dinner to be perfect, since it's likely the last Thanksgiving I'll ever have. The vascular surgeon took Jon aside Tuesday and told him I probably only have six months to live, and even if all the treatment I'm going through now is successful, and he says it probably won't be, at most I'll have two years."

She was shortly back in the hospital, weakened by infection and facing narrowing options. For several years Cheryl railed against amputation each time a physician broached it. Absolutely not, she'd say. Late one night she called and dictated a will for me to type and fax back for her to sign, believing she may not survive until morning.

She chose life and consented to amputation of her leg just below the knee. It might allow fitting for a prosthesis. It was in the midst of a circular journey between hospital and rehab centers that she called me one evening, beside herself because Jon was missing. He had an appointment with a counselor at the Veterans' Administration that afternoon and hadn't turned up back at home. I offered to make some calls she was too weak to make herself and found him, or so I believed, at the VA clinic. They wouldn't confirm it because of privacy law, but I gave staff the number to call his wife. He had been committed over a long weekend due to stress and sheer exhaustion.

A month later, on a Monday afternoon in mid-March Cheryl called again. She was in another rehab center. The goal was to build her strength enough to take the remainder of the original leg and amputate the other.

"Ain't gonna happen," she said. "I'll go into hospice first." She hadn't yet told Jon all the details, fearing he was not strong enough. One day she asked him if he would return to Washington State after she was gone and he started to cry. I told her to call me any time, any hour.

Cheryl left a message on my home phone on a Monday evening when I was away. "I hope you're out having fun." There was something in her voice. It would be over two weeks after she passed in her sleep before Jon notified me by email. It was likely the Saturday after leaving her message. I regret I was not there to talk with her one more time.

Now I picture her busy taking notes and photos for a new celestial guidebook. Her creativity and imagination left me in awe. I count it a privilege to have been her friend for many years.

What I learned from Cheryl:
Pay attention to everything.
Cry, then carry on.
Try new foods.
Keep imagining.
Be steadfast.
Travel often and far.
Share beauty.
Keep in touch.
Gifts of the heart (and stomach) are best.

Chapter Five

You want to know my philosophy? Look at my refrigerator.

Kathy

Kathy & Me

Is it possible or seemly to call a friend a soul mate? I selfishly want to think of her thus, even knowing that among her legion of friends, others may make the same claim on her.

Kathleen Quinn Weltzin and I never called each other every day. Though we lived only four miles apart on quiet residential streets, we could go weeks without seeing each other. We barely knew each other's husbands. That's not the kind of friendship we had. Why then, after moving three thousand miles away from the home town we shared, is coffee with Kathy at a local grocery store one of the things I still miss most?

We met over a shared love of art. When I moved to Juneau, I quickly sought out the Audubon chapter. There were no local art shows centering on nature and I thought an art show would be a great way to celebrate John J. Audubon's April 26 birthday. I enlisted help of the chapter president to start a juried art show we called *Artabon*. It was radical for a small town, ask people to submit art, then tell them it wasn't good enough to be included. I pushed for a juried show because I wanted guest artists from outside Alaska to act as jurors and thought they wouldn't come if it didn't meet at least a minimum level of quality. After that first year, when I let the president take the hard role of explaining to entrants their piece didn't make the cut, we created something that all artists aspired to and people looked forward to attending.

A few years later a newcomer with a similar bent came to our annual show opening. Kathy. Like me she moved to Juneau from Anchorage, where she had been involved in a far more complex art show sponsored by Anchorage Audubon Society. Kathy approached me on opening night and said "How can I help?" We both loved art as admirers and patrons. Her brother, Thomas Quinn, is an award-winning bird and wildlife artist who was already recognized and successful with what was then a prestigious Mill Pond Press.

Planning and attending art shows forged our initial bond. At first it was just *Artabon*. Months ahead we'd find an artist whose work we admired in the Lower 48, and invite them to come as juror in exchange for airfare and a place to stay. Kathy often had contacts through her brother, but procuring a guest juror was easy. If they were available, they always said yes. Alaska was still a place of mystery. Most artists had never been there, and knew that new subjects for their work awaited them. We selected a gallery to host the show and got the best downtown hotel to donate a room—it was in early spring, between the time state legislators went home and tourists arrived. We arranged for bird walks with the most knowledgeable birders in our chapter. I wrote a feature story for the local paper using the guest artist's name and portfolio to promote the show. Other Audubon members made trays of cookies and *hors d'oeuvres*; we brought a big coffee pot, then beamed at opening night like we had birthed this child.

Our tasks, Kathy called them. We made them happen through phone calls and a few meetings together. We both had day jobs and husbands, she was still raising three children.

Eventually we found reasons to spend time together beyond planning *Artabon*, and when the show had run its course—as all things do—we were firm friends.

It grew from there to span decades, often around art and Audubon activities. A ferry trip to Haines for a fall gathering of 3,000 bald eagles. A spring flight to Cordova for the migration of millions of shorebirds. Planning and staffing the Audubon booth at the Holiday Public Market. Long after the Audubon art show ceased to exist, we continued going to art shows and picking out our favorite work. I cannot remember a time when we did not choose the same one.

Her own home is a virtual art gallery anchored by watercolor bird paintings by her brother and impressionistic oil landscapes by his equally talented wife, Jeri Nichols Quinn. Kathy summers across the mountains behind Juneau in Atlin, B.C., a haven for artists. Each fall she'd bring back a new treasure, some acquired by barter, some through outright purchase. One year I gave her money and asked her to bring me a carving by Maureen Morris, one of her Atlin neighbors and an extraordinary artist. I knew that if Kathy liked it, so would I. She brought a graceful cormorant carved of shed caribou horn. How many of Maureen's carvings fill her own house? Kathy has no idea, she's lost count but they are everywhere.

The ambience and assortment of art work that would look cluttered or even trashy in most places looks exactly right in hers. Because every piece stands on its own as quality art, everything works together. A week would not be long enough to take it all in or appreciate every piece because each has a story to tell of her life.

When a Great Horned Owl perched on a spruce bough just off our Juneau deck, waiting for a blue grouse to fly within reach, she gave me an artist proof of the owl painted by her brother. It now holds court in the sunroom, my favorite room in my New York home. There is not a single room that does not display one or more gifts from her or mementos of our time together. Items that were just baubles when we lived within a few miles have become almost sacred now that we are four time zones apart.

Real starfish, a driftwood mobile with sea glass, shadow box, a starfish shaped candle holder all add dimension to my bathroom filled with seascapes. The raven refrigerator magnet painted by June Hunter of Vancouver elevates the genre to the stratosphere. A raven candle holder sits on the window casing in the sewing room/office. We share a love of ravens, in life and on canvas. A warbler painted on tin migrates between my front door in summer and bedroom in winter.

Kathy and I met for coffee in the Mendenhall Valley Safeway grocery store with an in-store Starbucks and nearby counters with croissants and sweet rolls. From their coffee shop seating area we could look out windows at sharp peaks surrounding the upper Mendenhall Glacier. How many places in the world could you go into a grocery store and look at a glacier, we often said. In fall we watched as the snow level crept further down the mountains; in spring we watched it recede.

It was the backdrop for musings about our lives, work, family, politics and morality. We'd talk about family—there was always something going on with hers. About politics, which were personal in Alaska because we all knew office-holders from the local assembly to the Governor's office. Whether talk of morals or current events, they included what she calls "snippets of wisdom."

"You want to know my philosophy? Look at my refrigerator," she'd say.

We talked about art, about her travels which were ever in the planning stage or just completed.

Though I called myself *Alaska Travel Specialist* when I was operating my tour business, she is the real travel expert, regularly traveling to places I'd have to locate on a map. Domestic travels, she said, were limited to seeing friends and family. The globe beckons her. Her travel preparations include reading about her destination in fiction, non-fiction and travel guides, months in advance. Plans for the next trip typically begin just after the last one ended.

After traveling to Belgium she reported that women were beautifully dressed, quite unlike our Alaska casual attire, and everyone was wearing tall black leather boots with heels. It was around the same time black boots were carrying Sarah Palin through her campaign stops as vice-presidential candidate. When Fred Meyer offered boots on sale, I knew I had to claim my own. When I had knee surgery, I fantasized about the day I could wear them again.

From her trip to Mongolia, I have a heavy fabric embroidered medallion that rests beneath a table lamp in my living room. People sold parts of their fabric to earn money, she explained. When I stayed in her home several years later, I covered up with an embroidered bedspread-sized coverlet, and saw a missing corner where she had cut out the medallion that she gave to me. She brought me a small cobalt glass pitcher from Mexico, a striped maroon and gold zipper bag from Turkey, white cut-out handmade pillowslips from a destination I no longer recall.

She shared her secrets for distance travel. Pack old underwear to toss at the end of the trip rather than wash, freeing space for souvenirs. Skirts are more comfortable for travel than slacks or jeans.

You have to keeping pushing yourself beyond your comfort zone, she says. When I traveled annually between Juneau and what was then my summer home in Western New York and fretted about the hassle of the logistics, she said that made it all the more important to continue doing it.

When her late husband confronted cancer, I was mostly on the sidelines with words of encouragement. Now I wish I had been there more fully, despite her insistence she was fine. Like many widows, she dwelt in the fog of loss for several years, yet quietly and within. As I was returning to Juneau after burying my mother, we met by coincidence (or not) in the Seattle airport. She had gone south to pick up a puppy after her husband's death. Weather cancelled our evening flight, a more common occurrence before cutting edge technology made landing safer in low ceilings. We found a nearby motel for all three of us—they always benefited from Alaska's poor flying weather.

In the fall of the last year we breathed the same air, she was diagnosed with aggressive breast cancer. Almost from the beginning of chemotherapy, her corn-silk colored hair came loose in clumps. She laid long strands neatly next to each other atop a tall oak and glass cabinet, a wordless mourning of its loss. Soon she was robbed of not only hair, but strength and appetite. When she could get out of bed she sat hunched over on a small stool next to the woodstove in her living room. Getting up to walk to the bathroom took almost more energy than she had to give.

It was my first close-up look at the effects of cancer and chemotherapy, and terrible though it was, I was grateful to share her life at that time.

I was working at home, editing technical fisheries reports for the Alaska Department of Fish & Game. After doing my work in the morning, I drove to her house each afternoon to urge her to drink water and to keep her company. I often took comfort food from Fred's cooking—meatloaf, roast beef with gravy, spaghetti. Divided plastic containers accumulated in her refrigerator and freezer. I do not know if she ate any of it, or it was simply too hard.

I made up a daily check list for the food and water she should consume but found so difficult to down. When even drinking liquids was an effort I made up a half-page check list: "Kathy's Liquids," with the subtitle "8 cups per day."

Flower glass (top of flowers) = 1 ½ cups
Tulip mug (filled to normal level) = 1 cup
Can of soda = 1 ½ cups

There were boxes to check each time she managed to drink ½ cup. Completing the form became a daily focus, routinely checked by the retinue of friends who circulated through her home.

"I wish I had a circle of friends like yours," her doctor told her.

Though I hope I never hinted at it, I did not imagine that anyone could sink so low and yet survive. Yet I never ever visualized her end either.

She must have been feeling better on the April day when I submitted my retirement papers to the State of Alaska. We drove to the Auke Bay boat harbor and walked the docks while harbor seals poked their noses skyward. Then she suggested we go to the University of Alaska book store across the street, which had as many handcrafted items from around the world as books. She bought a rainbow-hued embroidered book bag for her daughter-in-law and insisted I get something to mark the day of my retirement. I picked out a multi-strand necklace with wooden and turquoise glass beads. My freedom necklace, I called it, and so it remains. It was a bittersweet day, because it was one day closer to the day I would move forever from the state I'd called home for 45 years. And from her.

By the time our house was sold and I was preparing for my final flight from Alaska to my permanent home in New York, she was staying in Seattle for radiation, her last round of treatment. We arranged that I would stop for a few days to visit and stay in the room she'd rented. By then her treatment was complete, and she was packing up for her return to Juneau.

Her housing was close to the University of Washington and she suggested a walk through the gardens. Without comment, she brought me to the Chapel of St. Ignatius, an award-winning jewel of color and light and design. Alaskan cedar made up entry doors unlike any I had ever seen, the portion of the chapel that underwent more revisions and attention than almost any other part of the building. She knew my passion for architecture, and brought it to me like a gift to be opened.

In Seattle her goodbye gift took my breath away, another bird carved of caribou horn by Maureen Morris, this one a necklace hung on a black silk cord.

Kathy's love of reading is legendary, sometimes unexpected. She reads obituaries in papers like the *New York Times* and *Toronto Star*, not because she knows the deceased, but because she finds them interesting. One line stuck with her, and she decided she wants it in her own obituary: "She led an ordinary life, but to her it was extraordinary."

Indeed *extraordinary* does apply to her: wife, mother, teacher, counselor, arts enthusiast, world traveler, with myriad friends. Her children have taken up bits of her life as well. A daughter is a counselor, one son lives part of his life on and under the sea, another studies phenology, the effects of climate on the life cycles and activities of plants and animals. All married people of another ethnic background, a reflection of her openness to all. Surprisingly, given her embrace of the world, she did not learn another language. Perhaps it would have been too hard to choose which one.

Thoughtful. Kind. Encouraging. She always remembers her friends' favorite things. For an Irish friend who shares her first and maiden name, little glass shamrocks to slip into pocket or purse. For me, something with a starfish, polka dots, something white.

Has anyone done for her a fraction of what she does for her friends? Knowing that she also appreciates things handmade, I made a pillow top with a small kimono of mauve dragonfly damask, a nod to her interest in both. I woodburned and painted a plaque with the Latin words for "I am still learning." I bought a fabric holder for reading books in bed and sewed on a patch with the words from a stained glass window in Westfield's Patterson Library near my New York home, "He who has a garden and a book has everything."

Her house is filled with books she calls "my old friends" and she cannot bear to part with any of them. After I'd already moved from Juneau and I told her I was planning to write about friendship, she said she had a book to send me. She remembered a college term paper she wrote on the same subject in the early 1960s, when she'd gone to the Seattle University library for research and found *Friendship* by Hugh Black.

Safe Harbor

When I opened her envelope from Auke Bay, Alaska, and retrieved the book, I felt as though I should don archival gloves.

Gilt edges on top, ragged fore edge and bottom. Each page a work of art, the text framed by pale green-gray ivy climbing out of Grecian urns to wind around pillars.

Clearly this was a book you'd find in the rare books section of the library, not a reprint designed to look old. The copyright date was November 1903, with earlier printing in 1898.

"It was the only book I've ever stolen," she said. "I didn't want to give it to you. I went on Amazon and got you your own copy."

She sent *A Friend is Someone Who Likes You* by Joan Walsh Anglund. A book of Lighthouses. And *From the Shores of Ship Creek: Stories of Anchorage's First 100 Years* by Charles Wohlforth, history we were a part of when we both arrived there in the 1960s.

Friends are irreplaceable, but so are books.

Kathy also sends clippings. A column by Peter Jickling in *Whats Up Yukon*, "A Book is an Actual Thing," rails against e-books and celebrates the paper version you can put on a bookshelf or in a backpack. Her sentiments exactly. And a calligraphy ode to Grocery Ravens who frequent locales with food supplies. Only later did I note the signature, S. Isto, my former doctor who surprised me when she gave up a medical practice to become a writer. Surely Kathy knew I would recognize the author.

After traveling to the American Southwest to visit Cheryl in spring, my next trip took me back to Juneau, my hometown of 32 years, in September.

I met Kathy in Skagway after a five and one-half hour trip on the Alaska Marine Highway. From there she drove me three hours to her summer home in Atlin. After losing my passport in the Seattle airport en route I was unsure if I could even get into Canada, and more importantly, re-enter the U.S. But she remained characteristically positive it would all work out and somehow I sailed through customs in both directions. Soon we lifted above sea level over White Pass, into a golden September in the Yukon and then Northern British Columbia. After all these years, this would be my first look at her summer life.

Kathy has the gift of being gently direct about the most profound subjects without being intrusive or judgmental. That is what I always treasured about our coffees together over the years. Soon we were talking about losing a spouse—23 years had passed since she lost Jack, planning for our own decline, deciding what would still give life meaning. Getting rid of stuff. Keeping up a house alone. Having to make new friends when old ones move away or pass. The value of friendships with memories that span years. When Fred was dying and I called her in Juneau, it was the first time I could freely shed tears. After he passed, she sent a journal, *A Passage through Grief*, by Barbara Baumgardner. I again leaned on her with tears. And for several months, until she was off again on international travels, she called weekly to check in. I wish I had been as good a friend to her.

In Atlin I slept beneath a quilt she made of Jack's blue jeans the first summer after his passing. A friend in Atlin observed it was five years before Kathy finally began to emerge from a deep well. It was with tears that she finally took off her wedding rings, she told me, because "that's not who I am anymore."

"I have life and he doesn't. I'd better live."

On Wednesday, two days before our return to Juneau and three days before my birthday, she decided that dinner would be my birthday celebration. I walked a few blocks to a liquor store for bubbly white wine. She toasted my birthday, I toasted hers in mid-November which she would spend in Honolulu where she was born. She was in Hawaii as we were pulled into World War II. An aerial photo from that era shows her mother hanging wet laundry on a clothes line. Her family moved to Seattle, and from there Alaska beckoned, where she met her husband in Anchorage and both followed teaching careers. She lived through the great 1964 Alaskan earthquake, pregnant and separated from her husband by a mangled highway after it struck.

Kathy handed me a gift bag, explaining it was for me to decide who I am now, to take off and fly when I'm ready. I may need to put it in a drawer for a while, she said.

Inside was my third carving by Maureen Morris, a little bird with upturned tail.

I knew in some ways I wasn't ready to move on, that I wanted to stay head down in the world I inhabited with Fred.

That's okay, she said. "People want you to be okay but you're not. You still have work to do."

"When you're ready," she said gently.

Before we began the road trip back to Skagway and the close of our time together I practiced what I wanted to tell Kathy. It is the longest time I had spent with her in a long time. This week had been a gift. I don't know anyone who can move to the core of things so comfortably, so easily, so positively. My words did not come out as I'd planned, but I hoped she knew what I felt.

As time goes by, I miss her so.

What I've learned from Kathy:

Wearing a watch is over-rated. Just be in the moment and enjoy the journey.

Don't pack more than you can fan out around a suitcase.

Surrounding yourself with beautiful things you love is worth whatever it costs. Art may not be everything, but it comes close.

Coffee is best made with a French press.

You can't have too many flavors of tea.

Speak softly and people will listen.

Encourage others.

If you pass a bakery, go inside and don't leave empty-handed.

If something feels like too much trouble, it's a sign that you need to do it anyway.

Don't stay home too long between trips.

There is nothing like coming home.

Chapter Six

It's for you to remember me by.
Hildegard

Hildegard & Me

What a ride we took together through the magical world we imagined, created and filled with people from around the world, within a 20-mile drive from our houses.

Hildegard Ratliff taught me so much about life. Her street smarts outshined my college degree. How warm and generous she was and is, when her life could have shaped her in quite a different way. Earth Mother. Pragmatist. Poet. Technologically challenged. Too busy living to take time to write about it. There are many details I do not know about her earlier life, only how they shaped her into the person I met when I was in my early 40s.

The growing tourism industry brought Hildegard and me to the streets of downtown Juneau. Though we didn't yet know each other, we worked in the same office building for the Alaska Department of Health and Social Services. And we each wanted to shed the confines of a government job and work with tourists who came to touch the wildlife and natural setting that were part of our daily lives. We met when our new office became the streets and sidewalks at the Juneau waterfront. Cruise ships docked to disgorge thousands of passengers who would be the focus of our new lives. Each of us came with a passenger van and a vision for creating a tour business while sharing with visitors the land we loved.

It was her husband Jerry who initially brought us together. A tourism meeting was scheduled in Juneau Centennial Hall and he asked Hildegard if she wanted to go with him.

"Sure," she said. "We sat in the back and he pointed you out. I remember you wore a hat and a red coat. He said that you had a van and wouldn't that be something I'd like to do? What did I know about tourism?"

May 18, 1984, was a rare sunny day in the coastal forest of Southeast Alaska. When the Cunard Princess docked as the first cruise ship of the season, I was parked along the sidewalk with my 14-passenger red and white Ford Econoline van. One day Hildegard pulled up behind me in a blue and white Chevy Suburban previously used by logging crews. It was barged up from Washington State by a friend of her husband. We struck up a conversation that would last over thirty years. I had the bigger van, she had the bigger personality. She was first to recognize that by joining forces we could handle twice as many people as we could individually. While others saw us as competitors, we became collaborators.

Thus began our unlikely friendship. She's blonde, I'm brunette. Attractive even in middle age and beyond, she must have been stunning in her youth. She's outgoing, I'm reserved. She has a lifetime of relationships and experiences around the globe. I'm the product of a quiet Midwest German farm family. My move to Alaska was carefully planned, her move north from Denver was more spontaneous.

More than any of my other long-time female friends, we complemented each other and strengthened each other's weaknesses. Although she is nearly 10 years older, the biggest age gap of any of my close friends, I think she has lived at least four lifetimes compared to my one.

Hildegard defies her background. Many would have been broken or bitter or dispirited. She was a school girl as Hitler was amassing power and waging war in all directions. As life grew too dangerous in her hometown of Köln, she and her brother were sent to the countryside to live with family. She was nine years old when I was baptized on Pearl Harbor Day. Her father worked for the German government. I had three uncles in military service during World War II, but my own farm family was exempt.

War robbed her of the opportunity to attend nursing school as she would have liked. Pregnant and married at 17, she lived in Japan and the United States with American soldier husbands who were less than the partners she deserved. Hildegard came to America at the age of 25 with two children, speaking virtually no English. With children to raise and support, learning the local language was not optional. Television commercials proved her best language teachers; they were repetitious, used simple words and featured pictures of what they were talking about. When I carried some of her German customers in my van I had a tiny window on the sense of isolation borne of being surrounded by an unfamiliar language.

Despite very different backgrounds we shared a work ethic and built absolute trust, the foundation of all enduring friendships. I was the more serious and she respected what I said about the natural and human history information we shared with visitors and the regulations and requirements of running a small business. I recognized when she was schmoozing for customers, and knew she would never be anything but straight with me. I was direct about what I saw as facts; she could see that life is more malleable, more amorphous, not set in concrete. She trusted my intellect, I trusted her heart.

"You have to have a gimmick," we said as we looked for ways to stand out from other tour operators. Taking a cue from our vans, I collected a wardrobe that was totally red, from felt brimmed hat to turtlenecks, duster-length raincoat, chinos, and rubber boots. She wore all blue—rain hat, jacket, slacks.

She became *Blue*, I was *Red*, nick names we still call each other. We were two tiny cogs in a tourism business that grew bigger and more dominant before our eyes. With at least a dozen varied vans, limos and taxis vying for customers when each cruise ship docked, passengers were told well in advance by ship staff that if they didn't book bus tours through the ship, they would have no way of seeing anything on shore. When passengers walked past us on the way to buses they told us they wish they'd known about us in advance. It was us against the industry giants.

We drove downtown in early morning to secure prime parking spots for our vans, then awaited arrival of the ships together. The centerpiece of all our tours was a visit to the Mendenhall Glacier, Juneau's preeminent attraction for tourists and locals alike. Our daily routine May through September began with coffee at a café near the waterfront. Or with thermoses we brought from home, shared in her van or mine. In the years that followed, I spent more time with her than any other person except my husband. Time that never included a disagreement or cross word between us. Most days we drove separate vans independently, but after she got a larger van we could handle groups of up to 24 passengers together.

We shared an interest in photography. She had her late father's camera and called her tour business *German Connection Fototour*. We both took our clients to favorite photo stops, the best calendar-worthy views in the best possible lighting conditions. I could identify more native bird and plant species than she could; she knew how to co-habitat with bears because her rental homes were often located near their trails. She definitely knew all about fishing because of her husband's devotion to the sport. In the end, for all my Audubon activities, she was more comfortable outdoors than I would ever be. She ventured out in a small boat under conditions that would terrify me.

One day when her van was in the garage for service, she worked the sidewalks selling tours to fill my van four times instead of my typical two tours per day. She handed me a McDonald's hamburger for lunch so I could keep rolling, and refused to accept a single dollar from the day's take. Her outgoing personality made her a natural for sales. She always sensed when a little thicker German accent would serve her well, and I always knew exactly when and why she was doing it. It was pre-cell phone era, and we struggled in vain to communicate with each other by CB when our vans were in different locations. Mountains all around rendered them virtually useless.

When she decided to run a B&B in addition to the tours, grocery shopping, cleaning and cooking left almost no time free from the obligations of both. I knew that no matter how appealing it seemed to operate a B&B, I would never ever work that hard myself. After she and Jerry started wintering in Arizona and returning to a different rental home each summer, she transformed at least three separate locations into a B&B within a few days, always with charm. I'd read books and magazines about interior decoration; she'd simply do it. If I had an early morning birding tour I could bring them by for breakfast at her house, knowing they would enjoy the ambiance as much as her fried potatoes, cheese and sausage plate and fresh fruit.

If cleanliness and industriousness are German traits, she embodies them. When we led German tour groups in Juneau, she'd understand when one of the first things they'd mention was whether their accommodations were clean. And when we'd take them to an indoor salmon bake and they'd comment "the fish, it is lovely, but on paper plates?"

Near the end of another exhausting tour season I rewarded myself by buying the September issue of *Vogue* magazine and pouring through the latest trends. She would go into the Jewel Box and treat herself with a piece of jewelry, always something gold.

Most of her life she has had two or more jobs. At one point she worked part time for the State of Alaska, drove her tour bus and ran a B&B, all at the same time. Her B&B turned into B&D when Jerry went fishing and grilled the catch for dinner. Their guests were always invited to join them. When we met German groups at the ferry terminal he hitched a wagon to the truck for their luggage, calling it Jerry's Bags.

At various times she managed a restaurant in Denver, tended bars in Juneau, became nurse's aide in several cities, did office work just as computers were coming into regular use. Yet her demeanor didn't hint at the hectic pace she kept. Never did she act as though she was being put upon or stressed. Never short-tempered, foul-mouthed or disparaging.

It was her idea to always give visitors more than they expected, even at a cost. When one of my clients, a solo traveler from Washington D.C., was celebrating a birthday in Juneau, it was Hildegard who went out for balloons and champagne. Numerous times she bought wine and flowers when she learned about special occasions that people were celebrating on their trip. I was prone to save pennies; she taught me to go the extra length in serving clients. When I wanted to hurry, she taught me to slow down and listen to people.

She spurred me to calculate math in my head, especially when it referred to money. Because of her I can calculate 15% and 20% restaurant tips without using a pocket reference card.

Eventually they moved to Petersburg, a small fishing town south of Juneau. Jerry indulged his love of fishing from their remote island cabin and she traded tourism for work in a local hospital. By then I was arranging two-week itineraries for independent travelers and my days of hustling tours on the street were over. We no longer started every day together over coffee, awaiting arrival of the first ship. I had always been determined to outlast other independent operators in the local travel business—that old competitiveness. But it was her presence that gave me confidence and when she was gone I lost that brace. I pressed on, my life warmer and drier now that I was no longer standing on sidewalks. I'd sold the big red and white van and started meeting and transporting clients—couples and families—with a minivan. But I missed our daily camaraderie.

Her husband died in Petersburg, leaving a mountain of gambling debts and property in his name only. She paid off every cent he owed. "I could have been bitter," she said. "I decided to be grateful I was alive and could enjoy life. I let it go."

She returned to Juneau alone for a short time, but I was by then working a regular job with the Alaska Department of Fish & Game in winter and summering in New York. Her other friends were still employed and a back injury precluded working in health care. Her two daughters living in Denver wanted to bring her back to her previous home town closer to them. They purchased a condo for her and presented it as a surprise.

On one of her last days in Juneau, Hildegard and I headed for the dike trail at the Juneau airport. Rain and fog had dissipated, giving way to pure blue skies and a perfect day for a walk. It was a Sunday in late September 2003; summer tourist season was over. Fireweed leaves were bright orange, the trail was filled with locals and their dogs. Near the end of the trail we found a log at the edge of high tide waters to rest and to reminisce about the many times we'd led summer visitors on the trail for showy spikes of fuchsia fireweed a-buzz with hummingbirds, short-eared owls at water's edge, bald eagles in nearby trees, and the ever-changing intertidal wetlands. Then it was time to go.

We drove four miles to the Mendenhall Glacier for her last look at the attraction that had been the centerpiece of our lives in tourism. I took photos of her with the glacier and a waterfall in the background. The following evening she hosted dinner for a few friends at a Mexican restaurant; early the next morning she would board a plane for a new life in Denver. Other guests gave her farewell gifts, I held my own back. I'd spent hours designing a farewell card because I wanted it to be just right, to say so much. On the cover, a red stripe and a blue one, and a picture of us. Inside I included excerpts from the chapter on friendship in *The Prophet* by Kahlil Gibran. After dinner was over and the others had gone home I wanted to linger for just one more drink with her, but I knew it was time to turn and go. I handed her a plastic bag with the card, a musical CD with a picture of Denali on the front and a book for journaling. Open it when you're on the plane, I told her. I did not know if or when we would meet again.

It would not be long. Five months later Kathy and I flew from Juneau through a Denver snowstorm for a week-long visit. It was our first time in Denver and she arranged our itinerary with the same precision we used to plan our Alaskan tours. On our train ride through the Rocky Mountains to Glenwood Hot Springs I had to concede Alaska is not the only place with stunning natural beauty.

Seven years later, on a sunny Sunday in May, I made my last trip to the glacier as an Alaskan and moved to Western New York. The following year we both returned to Juneau in fall to push forward on a book we'd long talked about writing.

When I set out to write a memoir about being a tour operator in Juneau, I struggled with how to organize it and to summon the discipline to see it through. Incorporating her stories and including her as co-author was the impetus for finally getting it into print. She told everyone she met that she was working on a book, they'd ask when it would be published. It was the push I needed, and thus *Red & Blue: A Memoir of Two Alaskan Tour Guides* came to life. It was a gift to each other.

Even though English is her second language, she writes poetry in English in a way I cannot begin to do. She knows words in English that some native speakers likely do not. Once she was translating a German word for me and defined it as élan. How many even know that word, let alone translate it from another language?

Just as on the streets, her gift for sales set us apart. She sold perhaps a hundred copies of our book to my dozen.

Shopping one day in a Denver Costco, she looked at a day-old rotisserie chicken. Another woman bent over the same chicken.

"Maybe if we wait long enough we can get a fresh one," Hildegard said. When the other woman lifted her face, Hildegard noticed she was wearing an eye patch and asked if she had glaucoma.

"No, a detached retina."

So Hildegard responded with a story of when she had one, and how she couldn't fly home to Alaska because of it.

"You lived in Alaska?"

"Oh, yes. My friend and I wrote a book about it."

"You wrote a book?"

So Hildegard sold her one.

And that's how she flows.

When she spoke about Alaska at a luncheon in her senior center, some 70 people showed up. If she met someone and conversation moved to her life in Alaska, as it usually did, she sold a book. You don't try to sell them, you make them want to buy it, she explained.

Hildegard could have been wildly successful in public relations or sales and marketing. I sometimes wish she had followed those paths, instead of finding herself, in her 80s, short on cash and still doing home health care for extra money. Perhaps those routes would have compromised her integrity, and I would not have had the chance to meet her and call her a friend.

Hildegard intuitively reads people on first meeting in a way that is almost unnerving. She could tell what they felt, what they needed. She stops to talk and listen when many of us would just move on. She immediately sensed when a perpetually active widow was deeply lonely. She noticed when a young man stood by as his father-in-law struggled with bags during a family trip to Alaska. "He's spoiled," she sniffed.

Religion is an integral part of her life, though she does not proselytize. She and her husband helped found the New Apostolic Church congregation in Juneau. Begun in Germany, it still has largely German membership. When she returned to

Denver she re-joined a congregation there, giving her a church family and companions for hiking—next to religion for Germans—and German foods which she loves to make. Sauerbraten, sauerkraut, soups, German sausages, all find a place on her table.

When a church conference was scheduled in nearby Niagara Falls in October of 2013, she made a week-long side trip to our home in New York. I scheduled author talks for us at a library and a writers' group. I was too self-conscious to do it on my own, together it was easy and fun. And once again she was a marketing machine, selling our book to anyone and everyone she encountered including a waitress.

Hildegard met our New York friends and it was instant mutual attraction.

She has a quick mind and a ready sense of humor. When she met one of my pinochle partners and he said he had been in Germany in military service, she blurted out "Daddy!" They are within a few years in age, but the joke stuck and he is Daddy evermore.

"You must have been exhausted," Kathy said in a phone call after Hildegard was here. "I don't know that I could do seven days in a row with her. She wears me out. She gets out of bed ready to roll."

In November, a month after visiting us in New York, she called while lying in bed in Denver, watching big snowflakes drift down. She was sending me a bracelet, she said. It was the first thing Jerry had given her after they returned from the Yukon where they were married.

"It's for you to remember me by. It's bold—we like bold—and it's white. It goes with everything."

I heard her, but didn't quite comprehend what she was telling me. Shortly the white mother of pearl cuff bracelet arrived, with a note repeating what she'd said on the phone. I was left without words. It did not go to her family, it came to me. A symbol of the depth of our friendship.

The following June we met again in Juneau. Our New York friends wanted to see Alaska and when Kathy offered use of her Juneau house while she was in Atlin, it made the trip affordable for everyone. I asked Hildegard to come along and help entertain while I focused on the logistics of our reservations. She made it easier for me and more fun for everyone. We shared laughs and memories as we made home-cooked meals, drove to familiar sights, rode the ferry, enjoyed a picnic amid my beloved fireweed.

We've met several more times, in Denver and New York.

When I had knee surgery she came back to New York, helping me with therapy and allowing me to recuperate at home rather than in a nursing home. I've made return trips to Denver.

The Mendenhall Glacier has retreated significantly since we moved from the home town we shared; the town has changed as they inevitably do. Tourism has changed and grown to such an extent that we could no longer do what we once did together on the streets. We are still bound as friends.

What I learned from Hildegard:
Dwell on the positive, not the negative.
Think in the moment.
Always be generous.
Give people more than they expect.
Sprinkling hot red pepper flakes on pizza is really good.
Don't sell. Make people want to buy what you have.
Keep a sense of humor.
Smile.
Fold your hands behind your back.
Listen.
The foundation of friendship is absolute trust.

Chapter Seven

You can go through life and make new friends every year–every month practically–but there was never any substitute for those friendships of childhood that survive into adult years. Those are the ones in which we are bound to one another with hoops of steel.

Alexander McCall Smith

Judy Shuler

Friends for Life

In the full arc of our lives, early years create a strong imprint. Along with family, those friendships that endure from a very early age shape and color what follows. Just as Mary Alice and I date our friendship to earliest memory, so other friends have shared stories of their life-long friendships.

When I began spending summers in New York, I walked into Henry's Hair Co. and asked for a haircut. The first available hairdresser was Rita.

RITA & KATHY & KATHY

It's a cliché that friends make up the family we choose. For Rita Canfora it is that and more.

Born in Sicily, she jokes her mother was the first cougar.

"I was a change of life baby, one of the 'oops,'" she says.

When she was just 14 months old her mother, then 42, left the family for a man of 20. She was raised by her father until he met a 25-year-old whom, she believed, didn't want Rita around.

At the age of eight Rita was sent to live with her dad's cousin in Western New York. Rita was accompanied by her 18-year-old sister Rosetta, as beautiful, she says, as their mother. "They called her 'Liz Taylor'" Within four months of arriving Rosetta was married, a relationship that lasted until her death in her late 70s.

Rita would see her birth mother again only twice, when she was 21 and when she was 32. Only her stepmother survives—they video chat every few months. Though legally adopted by her new caretaker, Rita thinks she was ill-equipped to nurture a young child.

Enter friendship. Rita arrived in Dunkirk, NY, on December 2, 1963. She didn't know a word of English. She'd left behind her family, language, country and culture. Exactly one month later she was enrolled in third grade in Catholic school, an Italian girl in a Polish town.

Petite, with dark hair and dark eyes, she met blond, blue-eyed Kathy Koepke Dolce. Rita couldn't pronounce "Koepke" and called her Kathy Cupcake, a nickname she still bears.

"I don't know why we bonded exactly," Rita says. "She said 'you're the cutest little thing,' but so was she."

Kathy's mother was also named Rita; they joke that was the reason they became best friends.

The pair had their first sip of beer at Kathy's home when they were 15. "I think her mother knew," Rita says, "but she didn't let on."

Soon after high school graduation Kathy married, while Rita went off to beauty school.

Childbirth and child-rearing would occupy their early adulthood. Kathy had a boy and a girl, Rita, a girl and two boys. But divorce would follow, first Kathy then some years later Rita.

"We both married young, divorced, raising kids on our own. She was one you could really count on," Kathy says of Rita. They knew what it meant to struggle. Both bought houses on their own, without husbands. Though not close to each other, both houses are near Lake Erie.

"We cried a lot," Rita says. Both focused on raising their children; neither married again.

Over two decades ago another Kathy walked into the hair salon where Rita worked, asking "can someone fix my hair?"

Kathy Zarczynski, with yet another hard-to-pronounce last name, became simply Kathy Z. Pregnant with her first born, she had been going to a hairdresser who just lost a baby. Not wanting to make her feel even worse, Kathy called a different salon.

"It was Rita who answered the phone, Rita who scheduled me, Rita who stuck with me."

"We bonded immediately," Rita says. "I told her 'my friend Kathy and I are going out to eat. Would you like to come?'"

Thus was born the troika who celebrate each other's birthdays, holidays and families and regularly meet for dinner or drinks.

"It's just been comfortable with the three of us," Kathy Z. says

What binds them? "It's Rita. Rita's our main denominator. When we go out to eat she must say hello to 10 people."

One night, after admittedly a few too many drinks, Rita and Kathy Cupcake reminisced about the high school sorority they both pledged. Kathy Z, who is younger, "got jealous so we pledged her into the sorority," Rita says.

"We do get silly a lot. When we get together it's fun. We feel like we're 17.

"I can always count on them. I can call them at 3 a.m. and they would be there.

"I needed friends. I had nobody. They are the positive force in my life that I need.

"I consider them family. My children absolutely love them. My daughter has a Christmas party. She always says 'make sure Kathy and Kathy come.'

"We went through a lot of tough times and we lifted each other up." There was humor too. "We're not gloom and doom."

"When my Anthony (Rita's grandson) passed away I'd never have made it through without Kathy Z. I wouldn't cry in front of my daughter—I wanted to stay strong for her. I'd call Kathy and just bawl on the phone."

Kathy Cupcake was bedridden in 2006; "Rita would call all the time. She always checked in," Kathy says.

They can also argue like siblings. With Kathy Z "I get testy with her sometimes." If they're at a gathering that includes Rita's ex and "she talks to my ex-husband I get mad. You can just say 'hi' then stop!" Rita says.

"That's unconditional love. You can get mad."

"We all three think the same spiritually," Rita says. All attended Catholic schools, all attend Mass, though not together, all believe in God and an afterlife."

"It's hard to break it with the nuns," she jokes.

Rita and Kathy Cupcake are empty nesters, though all five of their children live in the area. "When the kids moved out, we began our life together," Rita says. Kathy Z. and her husband have a son living at home.

At a football game between competing high schools, Kathy Z's son and Rita's grandson were playing the same position on opposite teams. Kathy started talking to the coaches.

"They're like brothers. You can't play brother against brother," she told them. The coaches said they wouldn't play them that day. Rita was happy, Kathy was happy. And, she says, the boys were happy.

In the beauty shop she co-owns with Debbie Michalak, Rita is loquacious. Some clients drive an hour or more to sit in her chair. Children sometimes return a decade later, bringing their spouse to introduce to her.

"Rita will be here forever and she better be doing my hair the correct way. I don't care if she's in a wheel chair. I can get down," Kathy Z. teases.

"As a hair dresser we touch people. It's a whole different level," Rita says of the relationships she builds there.

"This is my stage."

Off stage, she says she is an introvert.

"Oh my god, I love being alone. I lock the door and I'm in my own little bubble. I call it hugging my house."

After talking about her friends Rita said "it makes you feel good. You don't realize how close you are."

"Tonight I'm going to call them and thank them for their friendship. I think I'll text them. I'll say 'I love you.' "

***

After admiring a friend's haircut, I asked the name of her stylist. She told me it was Debbie, who worked in a different salon. I switched from Rita to Debbie, never guessing that within a few years they would be co-owners of their own salon. Awkward.

Debbie & Marcy & Kim

Friendships that begin in childhood offer a unique gift. Unlike relationships begun in adulthood, they can reach back into early shared memories and find respite.

Shedding for a moment the grown-up responsibilities of work and family, friends can just be kids again. Teasing each other in a way only they can, laughing, giggling, having fun.

"We act like two-year-olds. Why do we do that?" Debbie Michalak asks rhetorically. "I don't want to be an adult. You can just leave it aside."

"It doesn't matter what you go through. Laughter is the best medicine."

Debbie and Marcy Sweetman were born to mothers who were best friends.

Marcy's mother was a beautician with a shop in her house, a favorite place for little girls to play. It was an era when women, including Debbie's mother, had their hair done every week. And it was likely inspiration, Debbie thinks, for becoming a beautician and now co-owning her own shop.

In grade school Kim Granata joined their group. "She completed us. She's like the comic relief we need."

Each brings something different to their circle, Debbie says.

"People think Kim and I are sisters."

With more rounded bodies they jokingly call Marcy "the skinny bitch." All live in Silver Creek, the same small town where they grew up, all have two children.

Marcy is a teacher now working in curriculum development. She is a history buff, "the intellect of the group. Not so much in common sense."

Debbie and Kim—"we have common sense, not into history."

"Who even won the Civil War?" Kim teases.

"You can't talk like that," Marcy retorts.

They try to get together once a month, Debbie says. "We understand life is so busy." Between shuttling children to school activities and looking out for aging parents' health care she jokes "I come here (to her salon) to relax."

They did family vacations—three moms and six kids. Marcy and Kim's children are college-age, Debbie's are in middle school.

Kim, a nurse on a Native American reservation, is the group's travel agent. "She loves to go places, she loves to explore."

Debbie took business classes in high school, already knowing she'd like to own her own business someday. Following beauty school she got a job in the same town where she works today, 11 miles from her home town. After working in other salons she partnered with Rita to open their own salon. Each was renting a booth at a different salon but unhappy with their situation. Debbie hadn't planned on owning a salon at that point but the owner of a downtown building wanted a long-term tenant. Debbie wouldn't do it unless it was with Rita Canfora, and she could work less hours. They've been partners since 2003.

At the time Debbie was going through a divorce and pregnant with her second child. Marcy had been divorced a few years earlier.

"You don't know what you'll go through," Debbie says. Through it all they'd check in on each other, bringing presents of cheer.

"Laughing is the best medicine."

When Kim's daughter was in ICU after back surgery, Debbie and Marcy went to visit her. Marcy brought flowers.

"Why did you do that?" Debbie asked her. "The intellectual one brings flowers and the nurse yells at us!"

For birthdays Debbie began finding gifts around her house instead of buying something. They shop together, bargain shopping.

Marcy drives a Cadillac, carries Coach handbags. "She likes the finer things," Debbie teases. Marcy has an enclosed hot tub with TV where they gather for cocktails. But they joke they can't stay beyond 9 p.m. when she's ready to retire for the evening.

Debbie and Kim are always cold, Marcy is having hot flashes. Debbie and Marcy like sports; Kim not so much.

"I think we've been lucky to do all we have done, with kids and husbands. We go to each other's kids' school functions."

"They're the first people you want to call when something good or bad happens.

"Old friends are the best friends. They know everything about you and still love you. They know the ick, they know the good."

***

I met Ginny in Anchorage when I worked for a newspaper and she worked in public relations. Eventually we both ended up living in Juneau where we had endless conversations about politics and shared a love for art and the written word.

Ginny & Mary

Some friendships pre-date first memories. For Ginny Breeze her longest-term friendship is with Mary Grisham Sinnott.

"I don't remember how we first met because we were babies," she says. They were born to mothers who were best friends, Ginny in February and Mary in December. Mary's parents became Ginny's godparents when she was baptized at Holy Trinity Church in Juneau, Alaska.

Younger siblings came along—Ginny had four, Mary had one—but Ginny's closest relationship with another person about her age was always with Mary.

As small children they played together, usually with dolls, every day. Their homes were just two blocks apart—one day they played at Mary's house, the next day at Ginny's.

At the beginning of fourth grade their mothers had them placed in separate classrooms "so that we could become friendly with other people!" When she learned that she and Mary would not be in the same classroom, Ginny was terribly upset

"As a child she was more of an introvert than I was," Ginny says. "And I state that positively she was quieter. I HAD to be louder—my closest sibling was 19 months younger than I. My mother gave birth to three children in four years." Mary's only sibling was born when she was four.

"In order to attract attention from my parents, I was more of an extrovert. However, my father was an extrovert, so perhaps it was an inherited trait, too. Mary's father was an introvert—much quieter than mine. So, in her case, it, too, was perhaps inherited."

Their friendship grew in part, Ginny believes, because of where and how they lived. They were so close because Juneau was an isolated community, and because their parents were friends. Their mothers spoke on the telephone almost every day, they belonged to the same bridge club, they did other things together. Ginny's family were Episcopalians and Mary's were Presbyterians but the two churches were located just a block apart. Juneau was a small town and everything was close by.

After high school the inseparable friends went in different directions. Mary graduated Stanford University with a degree in history and shortly married a fellow Stanford graduate and settled in Palo Alto. Ginny earned a degree in communications from the University of Washington in Seattle. When she married a month after graduation, Mary was one of her two bridesmaids.

Mary and Ginny each gave birth to two sons. Ginny asked Mary to be godmother to her son Mark, just as Mary's parents were godparents to Ginny. Shared interest in their sons, who are about the same age, is one of the bonds sustaining a friendship while living apart, she says.

"Mary has stayed with me through tough times, always there to help, never critical or judgmental," Ginny says. "When I was in a lot of pain before I had hip replacement surgery, Mary called me frequently or sent emails that said 'How are things going? Let me know.' She has cared for me so much over our lifetime."

While Ginny was going through a midlife crisis Mary suggested she stay with them in Palo Alto for two weeks while she took Erhard Seminar Training (est). Mary and her husband Joe had done it, and Ginny followed their lead. Ginny credits the training, and Mary's love, for snapping her out of her crisis. She got a job at Mystrom Advertising in Anchorage as the first public relations account executive and launched a career she never thought she would have. Eventually Ginny would return to Juneau to live.

In Ginny's 2017 Christmas letter she described Mary and Joe's visit to Juneau from Menlo Park, where they now live. Mary hosted a lunch for several classmates living in Juneau. All were born there, walked to school together, participated in social and athletic activities. During the luncheon Mary tapped her glass with a knife, stood up and said she was going to make a speech. It went something like this: "I want to thank you for your childhood and growing up friendship, for being with me through ups and downs, for staying in touch and for being my friend today. The end." Though it lasted a few seconds, her friends immediately teared up.

Says Ginny, "All our years together, although we often don't see each other now, came rolling back, and for that moment we were once again eight years old or 16. This was perhaps the most memorable day for me in 2017. Friends from long ago are still friends today."

Chapter Eight

Friendship is not a matter of the amount of time you spend with someone. Rather, it is a measure of the strength and depth of the spiritual resonance that arises between you.

Daisaku Ikeda

Spanning Time and Distance

When I first learned I would be moving to a distant town, I thought it would bring an end to my close friendship with Ruby Jo. But I would learn, as have others, that time and distance cannot break those bonds.

Linda is the daughter of my pinochle partners, and a childhood friend of Tina. Rural areas and small towns are filled with overlapping and intertwined relationships like ours.

TINA & LINDA & BECKY ET AL

Betina Tye Henderson and Rebecca Dikeman Lauto'o grew up a mile and one-half apart. They sat in the same class rooms, rode the same school bus. Tina's mother babysat for Rebecca's siblings.

But Tina's best friend was Linda LaVoice Shields. Tina and Linda were friends from kindergarten. They got bicycles together. Tina spent time at LaVoices' Bear Lake cabin. The girls were super close in junior and senior high school, Tina says; so close that when Tina's family traveled to Europe for a month, they took Linda along.

For 15-year-old Linda it was a new world. She remembers staying in a guest house with rooms above a restaurant in the little town where Tina's mother grew up. With one bathroom and no shower in the guest house, their party of six showered in the home of an aunt and uncle.

"They didn't speak English, we didn't speak German," Linda says. Mornings started with a soft pretzel from a local bakery. At night cousins took them to a disco where there was no restriction on drinking. It was 1974; Linda watched the news of Nixon's resignation in German media. She still has at hand her scrapbook filled with pictures, postcards, tickets from the trip.

Tina didn't cross the stage with Linda and other classmates to claim her high school diploma because she had a newborn son and lacked credits in English. She subsequently finished the required class at Fredonia State College.

Linda went on to college and married her high school sweetheart, Bill.

June 4, 1979 was a life-changing day for Tina, etched in her memory. She entered the U.S. Air Force to support her son, then two. Her plan was to stay four years. Instead Tina found her niche—"not so much the job as the people"—and remained 31 years, achieving the rank of Chief Master Sergeant, the highest enlisted rank.

With an IQ that could have led her into any field—she could have been valedictorian had she graduated—her recruiter directed her into open mechanics. She was the first woman in the Flight Maintenance Squadron's Corrosion Control Shop. As a corrosion control specialist, she ground and sanded aircraft. In early years she did experience some harassment as a woman in a man's world. She filed a grievance and got reassigned to a better job as result. Made responsible for 1,100 technical orders, she took them from failing to only two errors in six months. It was the beginning of respect that followed her through her career.

After starting her military life she lost touch with friends back home.

She met her husband in Okinawa, one of many places she would be stationed throughout her career.

Back in the U.S. at Hill Air Force Base in Utah she went to the medical clinic for a post-partum exam shortly after birth of her second child, a girl. She was picking up her records prior to her appointment when she heard a voice.

"Tina! Tina Tye, is that you?"

"I turned around and looked at this pregnant lady. 'Becky, Becky Dikeman. Is that you?' "

Tina hadn't even known Becky also joined the Air Force. By then Becky had separated from the service but her husband, whom she'd met at Eglin Air Force Base, Florida, was still active duty.

"We need to get together. Where do you live?"

"I live behind Lincoln Elementary School."

"I live behind Lincoln Elementary School!"

Their houses were around the corner from each other, nearly adjacent.

With babies close to the same age they renewed their childhood acquaintanceship.

Becky said "we need to get our husbands together."

Turned out they were in the same shop; in fact, Becky's husband was supervisor to Tina's husband.

They remained close but saw less of each other when Becky's family bought a new house in the canyon some distance away and shortly afterwards, her husband separated from the service.

Then, in 1988, Tina was transferred to Michigan and the former classmates, both raising young families, totally lost touch.

Fast forward 27 years. Tina was living back in her home community, headed for morning coffee. The usual local hangout, the Brocton diner, had started closing on Mondays. So she drove instead to nearby Westfield and walked into a diner there.

"Tina!"

"Oh my god, Becky!"

Becky, now living in Ogden, had come back to Western New York for her mother's 80th birthday and was leaving that noon. Again they had met by fluke, but this time committed to keeping in touch and visiting each year.

Three years later Tina planned to attend a conference in Salt Lake City and add a few days to visit her old friend Becky. Her airline tickets were already purchased when a detached retina grounded her travel plans. A month after the intended trip Becky's sister suddenly died and when she and her husband came back for the funeral they stayed with Tina. "God had a reason for their delayed visit!" Tina says.

Tina was also the first woman Senior Enlisted Manager of Command Center for the Combined Joint Forces Unit in Korea, working for the General over the entire Peninsula. About once a month she went to a women's senior care facility and orphanage to read to children at a school run by Sisters of Charity. She also sang in a church choir and met Adela Nicholson, a woman from Cuba sent to the United States under Operation Peter Pan, the airlift of 14,000 children from Cuba at the height of the Cold War in 1961 and 1962. They became so close that when Tina lost her husband eight years later, Adela and her husband drove seven hours to attend his funeral. They left immediately afterwards to drive the seven hours back so Adela could be home for thyroid gland surgery the next morning to remove a massive tumor.

Before Tina retired from the Air Force in 2010 she had battled back breast cancer. Little did they imagine that within a month her husband Willis would pass from a rare blood disease they suspect he contracted while deployed to the Middle East. Tina always loved teaching and had planned to earn a degree through the University of Arkansas. But with Willis' loss, she lost all interest. Twenty-seven years as a wife, gone. Her identity as Chief, gone. She had to re-define who she was.

But her role as a teacher continues to guide her. She was teaching Sunday School and learned the son of a friend had Asperger's syndrome, and the medical answer was more drugs. When another friend told her about use of essential oils for autism, she decided to attend a meeting to learn more. Parents had brought their children and Tina observed that none of them displayed the expected motor patterns.

Tina recalled her German mother had used oils on her children and vowed to learn more. She now sells essential oils from dōTERRA, and uses them for relief from her own rheumatoid arthritis and other medical ailments. She also used them on the incision from her mother's back surgery; even her surgeon was surprised at how fast the scar faded.

While Tina was working around the world, her school friend Linda raised a son with her husband and worked close to the place they all grew up. Nearly four decades would pass before they reconnected. When Linda's mother-in-law died, Tina had moved back to the area and came to the funeral home.

"It was the first time I saw her since high school," Linda says. After that they stayed in touch through Facebook and texting.

Linda was in Florida when her dad was scheduled on short notice for knee surgery. Tina stepped in immediately, driving him to the hospital, staying with Linda's mom, then driving to Walmart to fill a prescription just before they closed. Returning to the house that had seemed so big when she went to pajama parties there as a little girl.

"After all these years she's the same old friend," Linda says. "She's a kind, kind person. She would do anything for anyone."

Now Tina is a resident of Florida, living about seven hours from where Linda's parents winter. She still spends summers in a house she built on a lot adjacent to her childhood home.

Tina regularly goes to retirement parties around the country for Air Force friends, many of them thanking her for helping and inspiring them. Women call her their mentor. People who served with her could count on three things, she says: she would do everything by the book, she went to church and she gave everybody a hug.

"I'm the hugging Chief."

Hers has been "an amazing life journey," she reflects.

Her second daughter was five-months old when she was deployed to Operations Desert Shield and Desert Storm. Her husband was stationed state-side due to the baby's age.

After Saddam Hussein was removed from power Tina was tasked with editing documents for the Iraqi Air Force Command Post Operating Instructions.

While recovering from her detached retina she had to sit up in a recliner all day and sleep there all night for six weeks. There was no bending over, no physical activity. Her main pastime was facing straight ahead at a television set while relying on friends for food and errands. Linda drove her to doctor appointments and brought her meals, happy to repay the favor extended to her parents.

"I couldn't move, but I could pick up the phone and talk to thousands of people around the world," she says.

***

Jenean launched and led the writers' group which helped me find my voice and encouraged my every step in writing about friendship.

JENEAN & KIM

Jenean Roth and Kim Young grew up in Brighton, on the southwest side of Rochester, NY.

"Kim and I became best friends in about third grade," she says.

"I was always at Kim's house—it wasn't a back and forth thing, or sometimes me there and her at my house. A couple of times I got in trouble and grounded from Kim. I would throw a tantrum yelling 'it's not fair! You are punishing her too!' My mom's explanation always was 'she's the only thing I can use to punish you because it's the only thing you want' She was right of course. No one and nothing mattered more than hanging out with Kim."

Summers were spent at the summer home Kim's parents owned on Canandaigua Lake.

There were no secret codes, no "best friends" charms or bracelets so popular today, no spectacular adventures.

"We just were. No pressure. No doubts. Just best friends. It was never a surprise when I stumbled down her stairs into her kitchen on Saturday morning. Her brother picked on me as bad as her. I wasn't a 'guest' in their home."

When she was 14, Jenean moved into her father's house the next town over. Once she walked a half hour to catch the closest bus inside the district boundaries. Just once. Thereafter she walked an hour and five minutes to Kim's bus stop, at the top of the street where Jenean once lived and Kim still did.

Their high school was home of the "Chiefs."

"Ironically when being politically correct became politically correct, they replaced our beloved 'Chiefs' with the 'Patriots.' We 'Chiefs' are a dying breed, but just one more common bond Kim and I have.

"Kim and her brother were both adopted which escalated normal teen angst and parental tensions sometimes. She and her mother had moments of intense arguments and not getting along, but looking back it was just selfish drama of our age. We had a fabulous relationship with her mom. Her mom cared for us, took care of us and was always there for us, but not as a helicopter parent."

In high school Jenean and Kim dated brothers, the first great loves of their lives. The girls were left without prom dates when their boyfriends' sister got married on the day of their prom. So Kim and Jenean "went together and wore our boyfriends' matching tuxes with tails, short skirts and spiked heels. Years later I found out that's when a rumor started we were lesbians. Honestly I don't even think I had heard that word at the time."

Against advice that best friends should never room together, they went off to college as roommates.

"Everyone, and I mean everyone, said 'never room with your best friend—you'll never make it. You'll hate each other by end of first semester.' Not Kim and I. Not only did we survive, we became even stronger together."

At 18 Jenean moved from New York to Florida, "leaving her but not doubting we'd remain best friends. Whenever I came back to visit we'd catch up. Visits and catch-ups became less frequent over the years."

Jenean's father passed away when she was 35. "I came home to host his funeral and she gave me refuge. I returned to Florida and our contact continued to fade."

Jenean came home again when her mother passed away three years later. "Even though we hadn't had contact, in the tiny little town over three hours south of where Kim and I grew up, in a church dirt parking lot, I saw my best friend walking towards me."

Kim grew up in a business-oriented family. Her father was partner in a large construction company and her brother went on to take over the same position upon his retirement. Her paternal grandmother owned a family business, their namesake, Potter Associates. Kim took over that position and is currently president and CEO. Her husband owns a chiropractic firm.

"They are the nicest, most humble, generous couple I know."

Jenean was court clerk for the Village of Brocton, NY, and assistant director of Ahira Hall Memorial Library where she started and led a writer's group and spearheaded production of two anthologies.

"We track each other over Facebook, have occasional emails and have met up with other friends in person once or twice in the past few years, but I'll always consider her my best friend.

"We both laugh and laugh and laugh. We both are positive and love love love life. We're both there for each other unconditionally.

"We are both very devoted mothers. I'm a little more carefree than she and she's a little more cautious than I am.

"I think our friendship has endured because although we'd give each other the world if we could, neither of us expects a thing from the other. We are in our friendship because we want to be, not for any other reason. Even though we each have made different choices and taken different paths, we support the other. We embrace our differences and do not judge nor try and change the other.

"Every single thing Kim does is purely selfless; just being my friend is the most special thing she's done for me."

***

Mary Alice & Nancy

Nancy Hoesly came into Mary Alice Eisch's life in autumn of 1959. They learned, along with another 18-year-old, they would be three residents of a two-person dorm room in University of Wisconsin-Whitewater for the coming year.

"You can learn a lot about someone when you live in such close proximity," Mary Alice says.

Nancy and Mary Alice grew up on farms where the order of the day was the work that needed to be done. The other girl was shy and quiet.

"On farms, there is no room for 'shy,' " Mary Alice says. Nancy's farm was in far north Wisconsin—hers, a little south of middle.

Dorm life that year provided memories they chuckle about to this day. There were "gang" showers, where Nancy always managed to nick a leg while shaving. They lived across the hall from three girls who many nights walked more than a mile to the bar and came back drunk and frostbit.

"Nancy read her Bible daily, and she got a huge kick about the passage about 'heaping burning coals on the heads of your enemies.' She could think of a few people with whom she would like to try that!"

Although they never roomed together after that first year, they stayed close. Nancy joined a small local sorority with too few members to fill the sorority dorm; Mary Alice lived there as an "outsider." Nancy started playing in the band; Mary Alice continued band for her music minor while Nancy came to the concerts. When Mary Alice wanted to take her car on a weekend road trip, Nancy was happy to ride along. Occasionally they traveled the long road to Nancy's parents' farm. Once they told Mary Alice "Don't leave the water running when you're brushing your teeth!" Mary Alice grew up on a farm with running water for years. At Nancy's it had just been installed.

Because of her many years in 4-H sewing, Mary Alice was often asked to do sewing projects. She made pinafore dresses for Nancy's much-younger twin sisters, hand delivered to their house. When Nancy got married, Mary Alice made her wedding dress. Following fashion of its time, it was floor length with several layers. Mary Alice remembers lying on the floor for HOURS measuring and pinning to get the dress length exactly right. The heavy satin fabric resisted every attempt to cover dozens of tiny buttons that ran up the back—she finally took the buttons to a sewing store and paid to have them covered.

After college Nancy moved back to a house across the gravel road from her parents and raised a large family. Her husband taught school; Nancy became her small home town's "cake lady," baking and decorating cakes for every event—graduations, birthdays, weddings, baptisms. Even crocheting fancy starched figures to top some of her cakes.

Mary Alice taught herself to crochet about the time Nancy was planning her wedding. It would be a connecting point through the years. With the demands of child-rearing behind them, both now crochet prayer shawls for people in their churches or neighborhoods who are going through rough patches. Like the prayer shawls Mary Alice gave to my sister-in-law and me.

After college, Mary Alice followed a different direction. She taught business classes for many years as technology morphed from manual typewriters to electric typewriters to word processors to computers and iPads. She wrote user manuals for WordPerfect and traveled the country leading classes. Nancy does not use the old computer that her husband uses mainly for playing computer games. It is the only electronic equipment in their house aside from the TV with just local channels. She maintains that computers scare her. Mary Alice and Nancy stay in touch the old-fashioned way, with handwritten letters and landline telephone calls.

They see each other occasionally, but only if Mary Alice drives to her corner of Wisconsin. Four-lane highways admittedly freak Nancy out. Mary Alice comfortably navigates multi-lane highways and the 12-lane highway system in the Phoenix metropolitan area where she has a second home.

"I can't begin to explain the how and the why of our continued friendship," Mary Alice says. "So many differences, and yet, so many similarities."

***

Hildegard & Renate

Like Hildegard, Renate Kaufmann was a child of war.

At the age of five she was separated from her parents. Sent to the country for safety during World War II, she was unwittingly boarded with a woman who severely beat her for being late from school or slow with chores, and who ran a brothel and performed abortions.

She never saw her father again. He wrote her letters before he was killed with millions of other Jews. Renate did not know she was Jewish and her distant mother withheld her father's letters until Renate was 21, leaving her to struggle with her sense of self during her teen-age years.

Following the war, a beautiful petite Renate was courted by many but loved only one, an Arab strongly opposed by her mother. After a four-year courtship, her mother prevailed and Renate was sent to America to live with an aunt. Renate returned to Germany wanting Nani, her one love, to come to America with her. But he fell in love with another woman in Germany who resembled her, and Renate was too ensconced in America to leave. Many years later she dreamt about him three times. Working up the courage, she called his phone number in Köln. His wife answered; he was no longer living. "We both cried. I cried the whole week."

Renate met Hildegard Ratliff in Neusteter's Department Store in Denver.

"She was the restaurant manager and I was the head tailor," Renate remembers. "The year was 1969. Even though we lived 20 miles apart we always found time for each other which was not possible at work. I went through a divorce at that time and Hilde was my 'lifter upper.' There was always humor in our conversations.

"They say if two people from Köln come together laughter is not avoidable."

Renate lived in Rochester, NY, when I met her.

There she wrote a play as catharsis for all the sadness of her life, and as a tribute to the father who could not see her grow up and to the Father of her faith.

Hildegard decided she would travel to Rochester to see the play and visit her long-time friend. I was living an hour and a half away, and she invited me to join her.

We drove into Rochester, asked for directions twice, then stopped for coffee where a waitress brought us a map from the Yellow Pages to point out Sidney Street, our destination for Renate's house. It was a short distance down Main Street, a left-hand turn by a big bus station.

"Renate says it's the best looking house on her street," Hildegard tells me. "She's been talking to her flowers for weeks, telling them to bloom while I'm here."

It had been 22 years since they've seen each other.

"I can't believe it. We have so much catching up to do. Oh the stories, you would not believe," Hildegard said. "I was going with a guy and introduced them in a bar. I really wasn't interested in him but I told her she might like him. Well, she ended up marrying him. What a mistake that was. He nearly killed her."

"Has she forgiven you?"

"Oh we lived together after that. I'm the one who went up and saved her butt when she escaped from him and only had 40 cents to her name."

"Up" meant Alaska.

Renate's new husband persuaded her to sell her Denver home. They bought a fishing boat in Seattle and sailed it north.

"Neither one knew a damn thing about boats. They were nearly at the dock in Hoonah (Alaska) when he tried to kill her. He was drunk of course." Renate managed to get away and call Hildegard, who told her to get to Juneau with some fishermen; she would be on the way up to help.

"Later he said how sorry he was."

We parked on Sidney Street, a house away. Hildegard took out her cell phone and called Renate. I got a video camera ready to record their meeting.

"Open the door," she said in the Köln German they used in conversation. Renate emerged from the side door, cordless phone in one hand, while Hildegard met her cell-phone-to-ear. They hugged and cried and held each other in disbelief for the number of years that had passed.

Renate showed us through her house. "It's a home and a museum," she said with pride. "Most of my things are gifts. I got the living room rug at a garage sale. It's just perfect, don't you think?" Virtually every horizontal and vertical space is filled with kitsch.

Renate had invited us for lunch and brought out her home-made beef liver sausage, made in Ziploc© bags in lieu of the traditional intestines. Hildegard unpacked German bread she'd brought from a Denver deli. It was not the same bread they remembered—it's no longer made, Hildegard says. Renate asked Hildegard to bring more sausage from the refrigerator.

"This thing is packed. How do you find anything?"

"There's another refrigerator in the basement."

"Is that one any emptier?"

"Fuller."

Two packed refrigerators, for one person. A house filled with bric-a-brac. Her own bedroom in a third floor attic room. I think back to a little girl torn from her family home, with nothing to call her own. Do we ever surmount our early years?

Preparing to present her play has been stressful, she tells us. "It has been an experience. Last week the assistant director was hospitalized. The week before that, I went to the hospital with exhaustion. Last night, the director was abducted right outside of the theater door." She would later realize the later may have been a set-up and scam.

"When you speak toward the Lord evil always comes out. But when you expect it you can prepare yourself.

"On Saturday I'm taking you to Shabuoth Shalom. If you'd like to go."

We readily agreed. I asked her why she talks about Jesus but was going to Temple.

"We believe in Jesus," she explained. "He was a Jew. Look at the history. We want the Jews to accept him again."

Did she celebrate Christmas, I asked.

"No we don't do that."

"You believe in Jesus, but you're not Christians?"

"The Christians stole Jesus. He rightfully belongs to us."

She lives in Haifa, Israel now, a Messianic Jew. Largely homebound by declining health, Renate says friendship is "the greatest good beside Yeshua that we have on this earth. One must be a friend to have friends."

"We have the longest friendship," she says of Hildegard

"Hilde and I are of opposite character. She is a quick thinker, a super quick decision maker. She was always a doer. My brain works much slower yet we always came to an agreement.

"When just hearing her voice, there is a ring in it. I remember when I needed to get a call. I put my telepathic mind to work and in two days she did call. I believe we always loved each other and forgiveness was no hindrance. We are sisters in mind."

Honesty and love have sustained their friendship, Renate says.

"I thank God for having put her into my life."

***

Anne and I worked for the Alaska Department of Fish & Game, and retired on the same day. She gave me a retirement gift, a red knit cap and scarf to keep me warm in New York winters. Most people don't believe New York winters are much colder than those in Juneau, Alaska. But they are.

Anne & Deborah

Anne Post and Deborah met in seventh grade.

"We were both overweight at a time when fat girls weren't popular, and we hung out at each other's houses and went to birthday parties, shopped and tried cigarettes together," Anne remembers.

"I'm not sure if she kept smoking, but I quit when my mother found my cigarette stash in the box that held my 45 rpm records, and threatened to make me eat every cigarette if she ever caught me smoking."

Deb, as she called herself then, and Anne found different groups of friends once they entered high school and they grew apart. Anne didn't see her again until she graduated from college.

After graduation, Anne's first real job was with the Maryland Department of Natural Resources in the mountains of Western Maryland, observing and recording plant species and animals (mostly rattlesnakes) in a large state park. She remembered that Deb attended a small liberal arts college in a town near their field camp. Deb was on the five-year college plan and was still in school when Anne contacted her.

"I can't remember how I found her, but I visited her apartment and still remember how shocked I was to walk into a place strewn with empty beer and liquor bottles and half smoked joints, with Deb passed out in her bed at 11 in the morning. College had liberated her. She had changed from the overweight wallflower to a really fat party girl.

"I lived at home in Baltimore after that summer of field work to save money for grad school and continued to make the drive to Western Maryland to see her in college during her senior 5th year, but I'm not sure why since I was not a drinker or partier. I enticed her to try tent camping which she really didn't take to but she loved to drive and we explored the hills of Appalachia in her old VW Bug, often driving at dusk around curvy roads with headlights off. She said she didn't need the lights on as she could still see the road, but I always thought the main point of headlights was so that oncoming cars could see *us* and avoid an accident."

A year later Anne set off to graduate school in Idaho and lost touch again. In Glacier National Park where she did graduate field work, she met a man who accepted a job as an assistant professor of speech and communications at the same college Deb had attended. Anne subsequently went to visit him and rekindled her friendship with Deb, who was still living in the small western Maryland college town.

"The friendship that began when we were 12 years old continues today—54 years later. We had become friends in middle school, but why we stayed friends is still a mystery to me. She became an outspoken risk taker, while I remained restrained and quiet. She lived in inner-city Baltimore in a bad neighborhood, and ran errands, nonchalantly walking in and out of seedy stores, while I cowered in the car, fully expecting someone to rob me at gunpoint."

Both have made an effort to stay in touch through the years. Deborah now lives in Virginia and Anne lives in Alaska. They see each other every few years when Anne goes back to the Baltimore area to visit her brother.

"We go to lunch and drive country roads and visit wineries. She lived in Seattle for a few years and visited me in Juneau and was thrilled to see black bears at the Mendenhall Glacier several evenings in a row. Even though she's not an outdoors woman, she appreciates my rustic lifestyle. We both swore that when we turned 60 we would stop coloring our hair, shave our heads and grow out the grey. Hers is an eye catching red and mine is a boring ash brown but at 66 years of age there is no visible grey hair yet. We'll have to push it back to 70.

"She's honest, intelligent and direct, and doesn't hesitate to point out when she is annoyed with me. Yet she can be very understanding and supportive when I need it. We are both very liberal in our politics and lifestyles. She's quick to laugh and finds humor in almost everything. I guess she keeps me amused and retains an interest in my life and I admire her independent attitude.

"She's still a risk taker in a way that I will never be. Whenever I think of Deb, I think of the saying 'A good friend will come and bail you out of jail. A true friend will be sitting next to you saying *Damn that was fun*!' I don't know for sure if she's ever been in jail, but I kind of suspect that she has spent a night in jail for some minor violation or another, and I was always afraid that I would be sharing that jail cell with her."

Chapter Nine

Friends are part of the glue that holds life and faith together. Powerful stuff.

Jon Katz

Friendships Forged in the Workplace

I met Mary Simons in Juneau when I was planning itineraries through my tour business, Alaska Up Close. She contacted me about arranging a trip for herself, her sister and a friend. After I retired to New York we discovered we lived an hour and one-half apart. Now we meet midway for lunch once a year at Julie's Pizzeria. We both order the taco salad, spicy sauce for me, mild for her. She became a potter after retiring and my home is filled with her beautiful bowls, plates and mugs. All gifts from Mary.

Mary & Doris

Mary Simons and Doris Kirsch were acquainted as residents of the same rural community. But they seldom saw each other, let alone becoming friends. That changed when Mary became principal at Holland Middle School where Doris was a teacher.

"We shared many of the same values regarding education," Mary says. When she left to become principal at another school, she lost track of Doris.

They reconnected when Doris had a tragic accident which left her unable to walk, still both remained busy with their professional lives. After Doris was widowed, she needed drivers. Mary was retired by then and offered to help.

"I have been driving my friend who is in a wheelchair to meetings. She is president of the local Retired Teachers Association.

"I am short and her wheelchair-equipped van is high to reach. I found a tool which enables me to reach and close the back. I call it 'my two inches.'

"Doris had a little hand stitched, framed, embroidered sign with 'two inches' displayed and written in several languages.

How fortunate I am to have reconnected with such a wonderful friend.

"My friends are indeed my stimulation to living life to the fullest."

***

Mary & Marilyn

Like many friendships, that between Mary Simons and Marilyn Kurzawa began in the workplace. They met as educators. Marilyn worked for Boards of Cooperative Educational Services (BOCES) and Mary was a school principal.

Over 30 years later and both retired, they continue to meet at least once a month for soup and salad at Olive Garden. A glass of wine is usually involved as they catch up on family, mutual friends and anything else that comes to mind. They send cards frequently reminding each other of how very much they value their friendship.

"Not that we need reminders," Mary says, but putting it into words "somehow brings to mind how lucky we are to share this friendship. It's definitely important we also keep in touch by email or calling each other. I think friendship is something everyone needs to work at; it doesn't just happen."

As life-long educators, both value education. They share interest in theater, concerts and the arts. Family is important to both and their families are a frequent topic of conversation.

"We are very different in that my friend is a fashion plate and I certainly AM NOT," Mary says. "My friend is financially in a different category than I am because of her inheritance from her family. She is also a beach person and I enjoy wildlife more than she. She also loves to entertain and spend a great deal of time entertaining people whereas I do not enjoy that as much.

"My friend is supportive, caring, and always there for me. She has been there when I have had surgery, and when I come home she brings meals and is ready to stay the day with me. We have attended conferences together; one time in New York City when we were at a conference she arranged a birthday party for me. It was very special.

"Our friendship endured because we truly care about each other."

Mary shows her highly collectible nature-inspired pottery at an annual pre-holiday show and sale.

"She makes it a point to always come to my pottery show even though she needs no pottery," Mary says. "She is always asking what's new in my life and cares about what happens. In sickness or in health she is my friend forever."

***

What happens at the hair dresser doesn't always stay there. Debbie was cutting my hair, Rita was cutting Kate's. Conversation turned to my book about friendship and Kate volunteered a story about her friend Tammie.

Kate & Tammie

Kate Moore teaches seventh grade math in a town three hours away from the college where she earned her degree. Ten years later she is completing a degree in school administration.

She credits a friend, Tammie Edinger, for setting and achieving that goal.

Tammie teaches sixth grade English at the same school. They met and became friends about two years into Kate's teaching career. At the time Kate was struggling with her marriage. Both she and Tammie are driven and passionate about their careers, Kate says.

"We are drawn to people for them to inspire us or for us to inspire them.

"She transforms my life at almost every stage when I need it. A lot of what I model now is what she modeled for me."

Tammie gave her books, showed her how to be a better listener, asked Kate probing questions.

"My being a principal is due to her. She pushes me to grow."

One of the books Tammie shared is *Big Potential: How Transforming the Pursuit of Success Raises Our Achievement, Happiness, and Well-Being* by Shawn Achor.

"I thought you had to accomplish on your own but you can accomplish things only as a group," Kate says.

"My family is my group of friends."

Another book the group shared: *The Gifts of Imperfection: Let Go of Who You Think You're Supposed To Be and Embrace Who You Are* by Brené Brown.

"We're like siblings. We fight like siblings," Kate says. One time, when they were alone, "Tammie told me 'get the **** out of my classroom.'"

Friendship is irreplaceable, often inexplicable.

"It's your safe space. You can unravel, you can crumble," Kate says. You can totally be yourself. "Make-up free, haven't done my hair. Probably haven't showered."

It's different from a romantic partner, but no less mysterious.

When Kate completes her administrative degree she hopes to find work close to the college town where she got her undergraduate degree.

If she moves, what will happen to her friendship with Tammie? They've talked about that.

Tammie was in a new romantic relationship a few years ago, Kate is in one now. Regardless of what happens in that aspect of their lives, Kate trusts their friendship will continue.

"She's like my hub of inspiration so I'm sure I'll be tapping into that."

Chapter Ten

Friendship is one mind in two bodies.
Mencius

Soulmates

You have friends, and if you're really fortunate, you have a soulmate.

Haruna studied at the university campus a few miles from my house. One of her theater professors suggested I contact her for a story about friendship. By then she was already an instructor in the Music Theatre Department of Mahidol University in Thailand. Even by email our words reveal something of ourselves, and when I wished her a happy birthday on Facebook I had to remind myself we'd never actually met.

Haruna & Ryoko

Haruna Tsuchiya and Ryoko Hashimoto met in 1988 in Shimoda, Japan.

It was "in a classroom with wooden floor at a kindergarten," Ryoko remembers.

"We were one of the three new students to join the class that year," Haruna says.

Since Ryoko's family moved from place to place because of her dad's job, "we were living close to each other only for four years. For the last 22 years or so, we've only been in touch via letters, occasional phone conversations, and after the internet era, via emails. Since 2002, I've been living abroad, and it's been further in distance, and it's very rare to see each other in person," says Haruna.

Despite long separations that would erode many a friendship, theirs has endured because "I simply feel we are one of the very closest soulmates, and that our connection is a special one," Haruna says.

"It seems like we feel each other's conditions quite well—especially she is more sensitive with that. For example, when I'm feeling sick, she feels it. It's like we are connected telepathically."

"Although it is nice to see her in person, we don't miss each other badly, no matter how far we live apart. It is quite different from having a long distance relationship with one's romantic partner.

"Interestingly enough, we've never had any fights. To make a long answer short, I feel our connection is meant to be."

Ryoko is married and teaches piano in Tokyo; Haruna is a performing artist currently teaching theater in Bangkok.

Haruna names all the ways she feels they are alike as teachers.

"We both have similar teaching philosophy and ways of interacting with our students.

"We want the students to think during lessons, so that eventually, they can be their own teachers.

"Also, we both strongly believe in the power of words and thoughts. We are very conscious of what we speak, especially to the students.

"For example, if a student is singing and the note is a bit flat, I would say 'can you sing in a higher pitch within this particular note? Even this note 'G' has a huge vibration range within one note.' and I'll point to the edge of the piano key that is close to $G^{\#}$, instead of saying 'you are singing flat. Don't sing like that.'

"They are both saying the same thing, but I believe that saying positive words is far more effective and is healthier way to communicate especially when we have natural power dynamic as a teacher and a student, whether we like it or not.

"We are very sensitive in terms of reading people's internal thoughts, especially feeling 'between lines.'

"Also, we really care about loving-kindness in work and everyday life."

And "we both love to eat, art and music, and to talk," Ryoko says.

Their differences?

"I am the wild and adventurous one," Haruna says, "while she is much more cautious."

When she was in high school, Haruna decided she wanted to study musical theatre in a university. At that time, and even today, not many schools in Japan teach musical theatre at a university level.

"This situation, coupled with one of my childhood dreams of wanting to live abroad, I decided to study musical theatre in the U.S., the very country in which this art form originated."

Like most aspiring performers she wanted to be close to New York City. "I had a list of all the universities in the U.S. that had musical theatre programs, and out of that list, I picked seven schools. Then, when I was a senior in high school, I traveled to the U.S. alone for the first time and visited those schools with the help of my American friend living in New York City."

Although not her first choice, she visited a State University of New York campus in the small town of Fredonia. "After visiting there, I just 'knew' that was the school I wanted to come! And I'm very glad I went there.

"Whenever I tell Ryoko something rather radical or shocking about myself or my feelings toward something or someone, she always says, 'I can't find any words to say, but I heard you, received your feelings.' She had never rejected my confessions, no matter how hard it was for her to accept them as they were," Haruna says.

Haruna is a talker, Ryoko a listener.

"I have to speak a lot and in details," Haruna says, "but she can speak an event with a few sentences. Although I can be a listener when I'm talking to other people, I become a speaker and she is a very good listener when we talk."

If Haruna were to describe Ryoko in a few words they would be "well of boundless gentleness and love."

Ryoko describes Haruna as "precious treasure." She says the reason their friendship has endured "is completely thanks to Haruna."

Chapter Eleven

There can only be friendship between equals—not necessarily in social position or intellectual attainment, but equality that has a spiritual source.

Hugh Black
19th century Protestant theologian

Transcending Differences

Beyond seeming differences, friends find a common core and through each other discover new ways of seeing and being.

Chautauqua Institution is a 20-minute drive from my house, up the Chautauqua Ridge, past Amish homes, sometimes behind horse-drawn Amish buggies. A gated community, the Institution offers a nine-week summer program of music, theater, visual arts, lectures and classes centered on religion, the arts, education and recreation. Speakers, performers and summer residents come from across the country and even around the world. I met June through her position as director of development at nearby State University of New York at Fredonia.

JUNE & FLORENCE

When June Miller-Spann worked at Chautauqua Institution for 10 years, her peer group tended to be much older people enjoying their retirement years. Some friendships effortlessly span generations or divergent backgrounds. Or both.

Working first in the program office, and later the Chautauqua Archives in Smith Library, she began to form friendships with summer residents.

As years passed she built a solid core group of Chautauqua friends, both seasonal and year-round residents. Although only in her 30s, "our common bond was our love of beauty in nature, the arts and education; we were true examples of being Chautauquans and living the concept of the *Chautauqua idea.*"

One of her friends, Florence Norton, was in her late 80s and lived year round in a mid-century home on the south side of the grounds. Affluent and well-educated, she was a generously philanthropic arts patron. Her husband had passed many years before June and Florence began to grow their friendship. Florence was small in stature, June says, "but considered a giant in the community. She wore a lifetime of experience on her face which was softened by bright twinkling eyes and a sweet smile."

Florence's family history at Chautauqua was deeply tied to the growth and success of the visual arts and the opera program. An ancestor on her husband's side of the family had given a substantial donation to Chautauqua for construction of an opera building, Norton Memorial Hall, with the stipulation operas be sung in English to be understood by all. It was dedicated in 1929.

That ancestor was Lucy Coit Fanning Norton, who made the gift in memory of her husband, Oliver Wilcox Norton, and their daughter Ruth. A Union soldier in the Civil War, he was the first to play one of the most haunting and recognizable melodies in the world. Norton and his commanding officer, U.S. General Daniel Butterfield, of the 83rd Pennsylvania Regiment, perfected an old French bugle call into what we know as *Taps*.

"My friendship with Florence grew into a unique union of admiration," June says. "When we were together there were no boundaries of age or social class. Our upbringings could not have been any further apart from one another yet there was never any difference between us. We thoroughly enjoyed each other's company and what we each had to offer through our conversations. We were always learning about different levels of existence in a world of words describing experiences of the past, present and future."

One beautiful autumn day they shared a lunch of pumpkin soup, berry muffins and lightly sugared gingerbread cookies served by Florence on her porch. Overlooking gentle white waves on Chautauqua Lake, conversation turned to opera and the complexity of all the moving pieces to unify a performance. Florence described her trips to New York City and how she longed for productions performed by the Metropolitan Opera.

"Florence would begin to slip into her memories, escaping where she was physically located and transporting herself back to the moment of experiencing Mozart's *The Magic Flute*. The marvelous lighting as it filtered color and movement on the stage. The singers' costumes constructed of the richest palette of color and texture. I was beginning to slip into Florence's vivid memory reliving one moment in time."

Florence passionately described *Così fan tutte*, the story of two young officers, Ferrando and Guglielmo, and their broken hearts for sisters Fiordiligi and Dorabella. "Florence's eloquent description had the ability to transport anyone to where the opera took place in late 18th century Naples, Italy."

"Although my dear friend Florence has long passed away, the memory of the bond we shared is one that I have never experienced with anyone else. Maybe it was the contrast in our lives that fascinated us with one another. Or maybe it was the delight of learning about the beauty of a true friendship and sharing a deep love and appreciation of the arts. Today I continue to think about Florence, and I feel a strong presence of her spirit when I enter Norton Hall and look at the quote over the stage which reads: *All passes; Art alone endures.*"

***

Sandy is my neighbor. Every few months I have dinner with her and her husband Bob, at my house or theirs. She is a gifted quilter and crafter; we both spend way too much time on Pinterest.

Sandy & Michelle

Sandy Noble's oldest friend is Michelle Henry. They became friends in ninth grade band class in Northeast, PA. Both played clarinet and sat beside each other on the first day of band class. Michelle lived relatively close to Sandy's home, though they did not know each other before that day.

"We came from very different ways of life," Sandy says. "My mother was a single mother of two, which was not the norm in 1978, and worked very long days at a restaurant job. We lived with my grandmother, who also worked two restaurant jobs to keep our heads above water. Michelle came from a 'normal' family…mother and a father. Her mother was a stay-at-home mom and her father worked for a local, well-paying manufacturer. Though not rich, her family lived a well-balanced life."

"Michelle excelled at everything," she says. First chair in the clarinet section, good grades, always well dressed. "She could hang with the elite, wealthier kids in school and the upper classmen and even got to travel abroad with our high school on spring break trips."

All through high school Sandy and Michelle did together what kids do, going to movies, driving too fast through snow, enjoying what was in the moment.

After graduation, Michelle earned undergraduate and master's degrees in archaeology. She moved to Arizona for her graduate work, met her husband there and moved back to Pennsylvania. Sandy got an accounting degree through Empire State in one of the early online programs.

Through shared values they remain friends decades later. Sandy admires her "because she is true to herself and a real down-to-earth person. She could, in high school and still today, do and have anything. Material things are not important, living life for each day is what is important."

For Sandy, too, "material things are just things—it is life that is important. The road twists and turns and it is how you follow the road that keeps things in perspective. We share the same beliefs and feelings about many topics. We think a lot alike."

With busy lives, they talk to each other perhaps four or five times a year, "but I know if ever I needed help or just someone to talk to I can pick-up the phone or show up on her doorstep and it would be like 1978 was the present. Conversations and laughter come easy…it is like no gaps in time have occurred."

Though not a friendship where they do something together on a regular basis, "it is a friendship that is special because it is real and genuine."

Both advocate for stray animals, and have saved an animal or two. Their gardens have native plants they've shared with each other. When Sandy dug out overgrown foundation shrubs, Michelle brought her sedum, bee balm, black-eyed Susan, evening primrose. Sandy gave Michelle hostas and lily of the valley.

They also have different interests. Sandy creates quilted and appliqued wall hangings that fill her home, she works next to her husband in their ongoing remodeling of a house dating back to the Civil War and tends flower beds that surround the house.

Michelle became the mother of twin boys later in life. She is Chautauqua County Historian.

"She pushes me outside of myself," Sandy says of Michelle.

Both have sisters that are more like each other than they are their own siblings.

"Her sister and mine are exactly alike so we share 'can you believe they did this' stories."

The basis of their ongoing friendship: trust, acceptance, respect, feeling comfortable saying anything.

***

Michele and I are members of the Write Now Writer's Group. She writes for blogs, creates podcasts for her local library and writes children's books. Both of us contributed stories for two anthologies published by the group.

Michele & Marisa

Michele's parents were divorced when she was seven years old, and her mother remarried not long after.

"I always had a closer relationship with my dad, but my mom wanted all three of us girls to live with her. Once she remarried, we moved in with my stepdad and his three daughters. He was working his way up the career ladder so we moved around a lot—like to a new house every year or two and to a new school most times."

By the time she reached seventh grade, she was in her fifth school. They primarily moved to different towns in New York's Chautauqua County, but also moved once to Pennsylvania, about an hour or two from where she grew up.

"Because of my many moves, long-term friendships were not something easily achieved for me. I was sociable enough to make 'friends' at every new school, mostly because some boisterous girl was brave enough to talk to me and all the other kids found me intriguing as the new girl.

"But none of these friendships withstood the test of time and distance. Being so young we couldn't keep up with our friendships because we couldn't visit each other and things like Skype weren't available yet. We didn't have our own cell phones and tried writing letters, but that only lasted until I became a faded memory to them and them to me."

When Michele was 11 or 12 she finally got to move in with her dad full time, and she started seventh grade a few months into the school year. It would be her last move to a new school. The newly formed school had just merged at the beginning of that year, so many of the students were new to each other. Michele became friends with Jen, who was cool enough to be friends with a popular eighth grader named Marisa.

"Marisa was pretty, fun and dating the cutest guy in the whole school. Every girl envied her confidence and bubbly personality. Somehow, through our mutual friend Jen, I met

Marisa and she invited me to her house one day after school. I can honestly say I have no idea how our friendship grew but it started there and never ended. Before long we were inseparable."

They remained close friends all through high school, especially once Marisa moved a half block from Michele. There were frequent sleepovers and they pretty much went everywhere together.

"If I'm being honest, I mostly went wherever she did. I always felt like I could be my nerdy, emotional self around Marisa and her acceptance of me meant others accepted me too. When we were alone we were weird and did funny things just to have a good time. Sometimes we cried together about all the problems in our family lives. I think what drew me to her was her ability to be whomever she wanted, sometimes that was dressing Goth and sometimes it meant heading off to raves. She could transform herself in such a believable way no one ever questioned it. She was fearless in being who she wanted to be all the time and fully embraced her individuality."

Both are children of divorce. Marisa didn't know her dad until later in life and was raised by a single mom. Michele lived with her dad from the age of 12 and always had a strong male figure in her life.

Today they are moms themselves, each with one little boy, still living in Chautauqua County. Michele lives in Westfield and Marisa lives about 30 minutes away in Lakewood. Months and even years may pass without seeing each other or talking as they get caught up in life, but they always come back full circle. Once they met by chance at the July 4th parade. They're friends on Facebook so they can see parts of each other's lives and occasionally comment on them.

Their friendship has endured, Michele believes, because they value each other and have created a history of trust and support that never falters. They allow each other to be exactly who they are and accept it with open arms.

"When any big event or tragedy comes up I know she'd be one of the first to offer me a hand and I'd do the same for her. Marisa is still her unique, confident self, working for the Postal Service and being a nature-loving mom. I am a confident woman being my unique self as a writer and mom."

While both are family oriented, caring, non-judgmental, deep thinkers who longed to be accepted for their true selves, they are also very different people, Michele says. Marisa was more of a risk-taker, incredibly confident and super sociable; she was a "safe route kind of girl with low self-confidence and anxiety." Marisa was also more outspoken.

"I think we bring something out of each other that maybe wouldn't have come out otherwise. I know she made me feel more confident and loved at a time I didn't feel loved by some important people or confident in who I was. I think I gave her a landing zone to be vulnerable and free. Although she always had lots of friends, many of them just wanted to emulate her or date her, not truly know her and elevate her."

When Marisa was serving in Iraq for the National Guard she wrote Michele emails almost every day, as often as she could.

"It was special because even in the midst of such chaos and struggle, she thought of me. I have every one of those emails still saved in my email."

***

KHADY & ME

Khady Sisay and I sat across the office from each other with facing desks, both employed by the Alaska Department of Fish & Game in Juneau.

We could not have been more different. She worked with numbers, I plied words. She is from Senegal. I had to look at an atlas to learn that it is Africa's western-most country. I am from the American Midwest. I am old enough to be her grandmother.

Yet I was immediately drawn to her warm smile and self-assurance. I admired all she had accomplished. When Khady arrived in Juneau eight years earlier with her husband, who is from Gambia, she did not know a word of English. Yet she enrolled at the University of Alaska Southeast and earned an accounting technician degree and an associate degree in accounting technology. By the time we met she could converse clearly in English and held a job in accounting.

Perhaps she was the subconscious inspiration that later led me to become a volunteer tutor for Literacy Volunteers of America. I couldn't imagine how hard it must be to take on a new language in a new culture.

While I dressed in my favored neutrals I loved her bright colors and bold necklaces that carried her through her second pregnancy in great style. Her first born, Ishmael Jr., was then seven years old.

Khady and I worked in the same office for only a matter of months. Then I retired. She gave birth to Rama. And we both left Juneau within a few months of each other. She moved to Kent, Washington, I moved to rural Western New York.

For friendship in her life she reaches back home, naming Kiney Balde, a neighbor she grew up with. They were inseparable until Khady moved to the United States. "We are always there for each other," she says. As much a sister as her four sisters in Senegal.

While living in the United States, she has sought out other friends from Senegal.

"You always look for your community. You miss your heritage, your culture."

Yet even that can disappoint. Khady met a fellow Senegalese and carried items back and forth for her on annual trips back home. But when Khady needed something delivered to her mother in Senegal, the other failed to reciprocate. "A friend would not do that," Khady says.

A friend is someone who is always there for you, who has the same vision, she says. Someone you can communicate with. A confidant. Someone like a sister.

Khady recently moved to Seattle. She's working on a bachelor's degree at the University of Seattle, going on campus before starting work downtown.

She says she is not necessarily looking for friends from her own culture. Just someone to laugh with, communicate with, hang out with.

"Friendship doesn't happen in one day."

In Alaska she sold African jewelry sent by one of her sisters. The vivid multi-color jewelry that was set off so beautifully by Khady's coloring would have overwhelmed mine. Before leaving Juneau I bought a square wooden bracelet, enormous wooden ring and round wooden disc drop earrings that compliment my earth tones wardrobe. I think of her every time I wear them.

I like to think that if we lived in the same town rather than on opposite sides of the country we might sometimes hang out. But we have both discovered in our lives that distance does not sever bonds.

Only a lack of trust can do that.

Chapter Twelve

The greatest gift of life is friendship, and I have received it.

Hubert Humphrey

Friendships Among Guys

Images of friendship were historically male. A century ago books on friendship were written by men, for men. Hugh Black, C.S. Lewis, Dale Carnegie, all extoled the values of friendship between men. Carnegie's immensely popular, enduring *How to Win Friends and Influence People*, was geared in part to winning financial success in male-dominated business. Black's *Friendship* and *The Four Loves* by Lewis are grounded in theology, Scripture and that extra component in friendship they refer to as the soul.

Today images of friendship are more likely female. Contemporary studies show men's friendships are often based on shared activities, reciprocating favors and working together on projects. Men share activities, women share feelings.

Al was a high school classmate of my husband Fred; Bill was a few years behind them. I met both through the years on our trips home to visit Fred's parents. Bill and Al and their wives visited us in Alaska, staying with us and touring our favorite visitor highlights.

AL & BILL

Al Thomas and Bill Hipwell have been best friends for over 60 years. Al is older by two years, which can be a mighty chasm while still in high school. Their friendship began after Bill returned home from serving in the U.S. Navy. He joined "to see the world," was stationed twice in Imperial, CA, once in Guam—"never got on a ship."

Al has two sons and a daughter; Bill has one of each. Their wives bonded and while they were shopping and doing things together, Al and Bill hung out, often over a beer or two.

Bill says of Al "to this day he is one of the best athletes to come out of Brocton School." Al played football, baseball, volleyball, track, ping pong. After high school he tried out for the farm team for the Pittsburg Pirates. Al was newly married and they even offered to find a job for his wife while he played, but he decided not to pursue it.

Sports were their common bond. Both are admittedly competitive. They were two original coaches of Brocton Midget Football. The kids they coached are now retired, and still come up to say hello. They did a lot of golfing at courses around the area starting in the 1960s and used to play in scramble tournaments. Mobility ended Al's golfing. Bill quit the year he played so badly and said "that's it. Surprisingly, I don't miss it."

Both liked fast cars; Al once raced cars and motorcycles. They formed a business together, painting cars in Bill's garage on Pullman Street in Brocton. Al still has his '57 Chevy; Bill once had a '56 Chevy.

There were more than a few practical jokes along the way. Knowing that Al hated snakes, Bill found a realistic artificial one and planted it in his car while Al was at work. When both were vacationing with their wives in a distant city and met a purported boxing champion, Al told him Bill was a karate champion.

"You could have gotten me killed," Bill tells him.

In those rarest of relationships, they say there has never been an argument between them. They are "two peas in a pod. In a lot of things we think alike," they agree.

And above all, they share the vital component of all true friendships, complete trust.

This is what Al and Bill tell each other, this is how far they would go for each other.

"Even if you killed somebody, you are welcome in my home, no matter what the consequences."

"The biggest thing is that we trust each other," Al says.

***

Emory is my cousin. As he talked about playing sports and sharing a deer hunting cabin with the same group of friends through all the stages of their lives, their story felt unique and worth sharing.

EMORY & STEVE & KEN & GARY & CHUCK

Emory Luebke, mechanical engineer
Steve Gries, architect
Ken Koerner, business machines technician
Gary Sauby, firefighter
Chuck Witt, grocery store manager turned car dealer

Five guys, all married, most parents and grandparents, all but one retired. Tight friends since or shortly after high school. Through dating and getting married and the phases of life that followed, they continued to make space for each other in their lives.

"Cars, laughter and beer are the common denominator that kept us together," Emory says.

It was more than that, of course. What cements a friendship over decades, through everything else that distracts throughout life?

"We care about each other, laugh a lot and look forward to spending time together.

"We don't always agree, but we accommodate each other's views."

They started out playing basketball–gave it up when they finally realized they just plain lacked aptitude. They moved on to softball and volleyball and started, in a state where it verges on religion, hunting together. Deer, naturally, and pheasant and turkey. It was less about the hunting and more about the comradery and spending time together.

Their friendships began, as many relationships do, by happenstance. In eighth grade shop class students were assigned four to a table, in alphabetical order by last name. Emory Luebke shared a table with John MacDonald and they soon connected. After graduation John went into the Army. Emory went on to school, and bought John's Mustang. When

John came home on leave he invited Emory to join him at a local dance hall. There Emory met three of John's childhood friends—Gary, Steve and Chuck.

When John returned to the service, the four back home began bonding around their shared love of cars, camping and hunting. Ken knew everyone but Emory; he re-joined the core group after leaving the Navy

More happenstance. Ken went to a fish fry hoping to meet up with a girl he fancied. Kathy went to the same restaurant/bar looking for a specific guy. As the young like company, Ken asked Emory to go with him; Kathy invited Trudie. Neither of the invitees were much in the mood for the outing but reluctantly went along with their friend. When both Ken and Kathy failed to find the person they hoped to see, they started talking to each other.

Left on their own, ignored by the friends who failed to introduce them to each other, Emory finally asked Trudie to dance. Now they are dancing into their fourth decade of marriage.

As one by one guys started getting married they agreed they would get together once a week for softball in summer, volleyball in winter. Over the years volleyball and softball gave way to golf and bowling.

And "there's always a couple of beers involved."

Hunting and fishing continues. They bought 50 acres of hunting land together, first staying in an old school bus made into a camper, then graduating to a cabin.

Ironically John, who originally brought all of them together, has dropped from sight.

It takes some initiative, some effort to keep people getting together, Emory says.

Wives are included in their activities a half dozen times a year. Though they like each other, they haven't formed into a friendship circle of their own. Even during the years of raising young children, the guys continued their regular contact.

Common factor, Emory thinks: "we cared about each other. It made you want to stick together. We all were successful in our careers, but no one had such a big ego that you couldn't appreciate what the other person was doing, nor did you have to top the other person. We also could and did tell each other our troubles and could count on a supportive ear."

He feels their long-term friendship is not the norm for guys. But it was likely helped by them all staying in the same area.

"If I'd taken a transfer (he worked for a major corporation where that was an option) and come back, would it have been the same? I don't know."

Once they stood in each other's weddings, now they are there for funerals of each other's parents, the milestones of children and grandchildren.

"The biggest thing is the fun we have. We always look forward to the laughter."

***

David is my financial adviser. He and his wife also come to my annual Kentucky Derby party.

Dave & Joe

Almost any given morning you'll find David Zambotti and Joe Spayer meeting for coffee at Tim Hortons.

They talk or meet almost every day, except when one is on vacation or otherwise tied up.

"I'll be sitting at the mall, doing nothing. I'll give him a call," Joe says.

"My wife is jealous," Dave quips. "She says 'you spend more time with him than with me.' I say I like him better."

"We're the odd couple. He's the neat one," says Joe, tall, thin with graying dark brown hair and blue eyes, sporting retirement shorts and tee-shirt. Dave, still working as financial adviser, even in June wears white long-sleeved dress shirt and necktie. He is shorter, rounded, with thick all-white hair. They agree their relationship is probably unique among men.

Dave married first, and he and his wife Marie introduced Joe to his future wife Janice. When Dave's employer closed shop, Joe's father helped him find another job. And on it goes.

Both have two children, a son and a daughter, and are hands-on grandparents.

They stood up in each other's wedding, three years apart, and are godparent to each other's children.

"We're on the same wave length on lots of stuff," Joe says. "Cars, hunting, building and remodeling houses." Both built their own houses. Joe started one-half year ahead of Dave.

"It boils down to complimentary skills," Dave says. "He doesn't like getting down to fine points. I do. We talk things out and work out how to do something."

David and Joe met in a mandatory seventh grade choir. They stood in the back row, next to each other.

"I asked if he was a bass, he didn't know what that meant."

Joe's family had a rural camp, a building made of old doors with windows as walls. There was a wood stove, no insulation, a perfect place for teens to hang out.

"He said 'you want to come up? We're having spaghetti,' " Dave remembers. "Hey, I'm Italian. What do you say?"

It was the beginning of their lives with many parallels.

They hung out at the camp winter and summer.

Both lived on Lakeshore Drive along Lake Erie. They rode their bicycles between their houses. When Dave's father died at a young age, Joe's father became a father to David as well.

Both worked weekends in a commissary on the same Lake Shore Drive. Dave worked in a bakery with his mother, making apple turnovers, stuffing theirs extra full. Lots of chocolate chip cookies and turnovers sweetened their young lives.

After graduation in accounting, Joe had student loans to pay. His first job, as police officer in Fredonia, lasted five years, at $7,000 per year. Then he got a job at the local steel plant when he realized he could make money faster to pay loans. Joe credits his dad with a hard work ethic—even then he thought about retirement. Joe subsequently got a security job at Niagara Mohawk Power Corporation, then worked in maintenance and instrument control. He started there in 1978, worked there 33 years before retiring.

Meanwhile, Dave was drafted into military service from business college. Before he had to report for duty, they were riding Hondas, Joe ahead of Dave, outside an unfamiliar town. Joe came to a stop sign in town and looked behind him.

"Where's Dave?"

Joe backtracked to a road with a 90 degree bend, found his Honda but no sign of Dave. His face split open, Dave had gone to a nearby house for help. The scar is still visible, a separated shoulder still bothers him. When Dave reported to Buffalo for draft he was rejected.

"Damaged goods."

Dave rode the bus back home. He couldn't get back in school because the fall semester was underway, so he got a job at the steel plant. Already making more money than his father, he never returned to school. He got a job as water treatment operator in a nearby small town, moved there as requirement for the job and began building his house there. After eight years he went to work with a plant that printed comics for newspapers until they closed. Through Joe's dad he got a job with an insurance company, then worked as an independent financial consultant when that company no longer had employees.

Through the years they have talked on the phone or met for coffee almost every day. Often, both.

If they found themselves living in different areas, they can't imagine the daily phone calls would end.

***

Ed came to our writer's group to share a copy of his book, *Cat vs. Dog*, a series of whimsical cartoons depicting what goes on inside the minds of a cat, Clawde, and a dog, Fang. Each believes, naturally, they are the superior pet.

Ed & Dean

Dean Fowler and his family moved to Fredonia, NY, from Canada and bought a house in Edward McClenathan's neighborhood.

Some friendships form quickly. What starts as an unremarkable day leads to lifelong friendship.

"I may have been his first friend in his new country," Ed says. They were both about to begin high school together. Dean and Ed hit it off right away. They played a lot of sandlot sports that summer and having Dean as a friend held an extra bonus for Ed.

Dean's family began a business dynasty that continues to this day and is well-known at carnivals, fairs and festivals all over as Fowler's Taffy. In addition to his mother and father, it included older brothers George, Jack and Don, and one sister near his own age, Estelle.

They were an integral part of the carnival world, so Dean's carnival friends gave the boys extra time on the rides. For Ed it was like being given a key to the city except in this case, it was a key to midway amusements.

Ed was fascinated by the spectacle of watching taffy made in endless flavors right on the midway. Using a special hook fastened to a post at their colorful stands, the malleable taffy ingredients were kneaded and pulled with a "Will Rogers" lasso technique till the taffy was pulled to the perfect consistency, he remembers. Then it would be cut into chunks and neatly wrapped for sale.

"But there was more to Dean than that," Ed says. "He was an exceptional person in his own right. He had what Harvard professor Howard Gardner would classify as special Bodily-Kinesthetic Intelligence. He could throw objects with unerring accuracy, he could pole vault, he could ice skate like a hockey player. He could have been a star athlete." But when he turned sixteen he left it behind.

Ed vividly remembers their last day of school. They were walking home, just crossing the Canadaway Creek bridge, when Dean stopped at the rail.

Dean took his battered algebra textbook and winding up with his fantastic pitching arm, tossed it down the fast-flowing creek like a Frisbee.

"I didn't see it coming. But I wasn't at all surprised. Dean was always full of surprises."

It marked the end of Dean's schooling and the beginning of his entrance into his family's business.

Their lives went separate ways. Ed's schooling continued, Dean began his working career traveling the circuits. Despite that, their unending friendship remained strong. They saw each other intermittently during the summer fair season, re-living and enjoying memories.

As Fowler Taffy continues, sons, grandsons, cousins are all in the business. Dean's son, Denny, can be found in the familiar Fowler stand on the midway during Chautauqua County Fair.

"He is gone now, but as long as I live, my friend Dean, I will never forget."

***

Fred & Lloyd

When Fred Shuler was 14, his father moved the family from a home in Buffalo to a rural area 40 miles west.

Freshman year is not an easy time to leave friends and a school of several hundred students per class for a class of less than 50. He was the new kid who dressed differently, wearing slacks with a crease instead of jeans; he knew nothing of country life and ways. Stared at, sized up by the girls, he felt out of place. Every weekend he took a bus back to Buffalo to stay with the family of a fellow pianist.

One of the first classmates in his new school to accept him as a friend was Lloyd Corell.

Eventually he would become part of a close-knit class that remained tight for decades.

After high school, Lloyd flew for the U.S. Navy for seven years, then settled just a village away from where he grew up. Fred graduated business school, served two years in the U.S. Army, worked in banking, then went to Tacoma to visit a former classmate. He kept seeing signs for Alaska, and on a lark took a flight to the state that would become his home for the next 45 years. We met and married there. Our trips back home to visit our parents every few years invariably included a visit with Lloyd, his wife Barb and their three children.

As Fred's parents aged, visits home became more frequent and longer. When his parents could no longer drive to the airport to pick us up, and after they passed, Lloyd provided the hour-long airport shuttle. Through the years there were Barb's baked goods and peach jam, class reunion lunches, visits in their home as their children grew up and they helped raise grandchildren.

Lloyd was a kidder, a tease who was fun to be around. Though their time together was limited after high school, the bond they shared was strong. When something important was going on in his life, Lloyd called Fred.

After fighting prostate cancer into remission for 12 years and battling for years the weak heart he inherited from his father, Lloyd called Fred on a Thursday evening. He'd been feeling a strain but attributed it to yard work, trimming trees and clearing branches. Swallowing was difficult. Finally after a trip to the emergency room he was diagnosed with lymphoma, the easiest cancer to cure, he was told.

An appointment at Roswell Park Cancer Center was delayed for lack of immediate open appointments. After a biopsy and its analysis were further delayed, results finally revealed another form of cancer in stage four. It was roaring through his body. Fred and I stopped by the house every few days, to lift his mind from himself and give Barb a break. He visibly deteriorated by the day, adding some urgency to our visits. On one visit, Fred told Lloyd he loved him, and Lloyd said Fred was his best friend. When his daughter Kathy arrived from another state and his two sons, Doug and Charlie, stopped by more often, we backed off some but continued to stop by periodically. We didn't want to intrude, but I recalled the times I'd shied away from death around friends and regretted it later. And I remembered how precious was every contact when my brother was dying of cancer.

We went to town for errands, then called Barb to ask if it would be a good time to stop. The family was all in the kitchen, she said. Would tomorrow be better, I asked.

"I don't know, he's failing fast." She said it would be all right to stop; we felt it might be the last time. As we pulled into the yard, Doug was retrieving papers from his car and said he only had a few hours left.

We went into the house, went briefly to his side where he was heavy on morphine and breathing with difficulty. We spoke a few words, said we were thinking about him. Not knowing what else to say, I talked about the winds whipping Lake Erie into whitecaps. He did not respond, but I remembered that hearing may remain when other senses fail.

Then we retreated into the kitchen. We had brought them a loaf of zucchini bread from our freezer. I asked Kathy what I could do for Barb after he was gone.

"I worry about her spending too much time in the house alone," she said. I promised I'd do what I could to get her out.

Charlie came in from the living room and urgently summoned everyone to Lloyd's side while we quickly left to give them privacy. We were backing the car from the yard when Doug opened the living room door and said "he's gone." It was humbling to know that other than family, we were the last there at the end.

He passed on Barb's birthday. A few days earlier he told his daughter and granddaughter that he was ruining her birthday and he wanted them to get her a birthday present from him.

"What should we get?"

"A beautiful necklace." Something with a leaf because it is fall.

They went to the jewelry store Barb and Lloyd had patronized for years, selecting a small gold leaf in the scale the petite Barbara has always favored. Then they took a photo before wrapping it to show him the day before her birthday.

"It's beautiful," he said, a tear sliding down.

Two days later we picked up the morning newspaper from across the street to see when and where the funeral service would be. The lengthy article talked about his interests, his military service, his work, his family. Listed among the survivors, after his widow, children and grandchildren and siblings, was his life-long friend, Fred Shuler, with me in parentheses. I was taken aback. I've seen pets listed, companions who were spousal equivalents, but never a classmate who had lived away for decades. Would other friends feel slighted, wondering why Fred and not them?

Did the family choose to include us because at the end, we stopped every few days when others did not or could not? I know how grateful I was for every outsider who did something for our family, for my parents and brother, in their last days. It feels like a validation that even outside of the family this was someone who mattered. Of course you're there for your family members; friends don't have to be there but they are.

Or was listing Fred something Lloyd had requested? When he got the initial diagnosis for return of his cancer, he called Fred even before he told his family—he wanted more specific information before worrying them, he said.

Fred said they always had a strong bond. Both played music and sang together during high school; a common interest is the foundation of many friendships. But there is clearly something more, something elusive, so powerful that it spans distance and years and extends even to last moments here and beyond.

A steady stream of visitors came to the memorial service for over two hours, testament to the wide circle of friends and acquaintances of both Lloyd and Barb. Fred held my hand through the service. He had begun putting more accounts in my name and often told me to be the driver on short trips around town. He said he felt vulnerable and the feeling only grew stronger with deaths close around him.

That fall Fred felt a lingering pain in the side that he attributed to moving garden hoses into the garage and lifting them overhead. Just over a month after Lloyd's passing, he was diagnosed with squamous cell lung cancer; five weeks later he too would pass.

The nearly life-long friends were together again.

Chapter Thirteen

Can men and women be just friends? In many cases, the answer is no.

Jeremy Nicholson M.S.W, Ph.D.

Men and Women as Friends

Unrealistic. Unlikely. Unacceptable to at least one of the individuals involved. There is research that says friendship between a man and a woman, friendship and nothing more, is all of the above. But some set their own rules and succeed in building relationships that work for them.

We met Des shortly after we moved to Anchorage. Fred was hiring personnel as operations officer for Matanuska Valley Bank, she ran an employment agency that referred applicants. The business relationship grew into lifelong friendship.

Des was our window into all things Greek. We were graciously accepted into her family circle, enjoyed the baklava and spanakopita (Greek spinach pie) made by her mother with homemade phyllo dough, drank Metaxa, learned a few dirty words.

We saw her through divorce and remarriage, wrenching loss of her brother, creation and success of employment and retail businesses. She was loyal, driven, vibrant and full of life. One I was in awe to call a friend. We shared love of our dogs, we shared holidays, we shared a penchant for getting dressed up, which she successfully marketed in her high end dress shop in a town where dressing down was a matter of pride.

After I started a tour business in Juneau, she and her husband bought a tour business in Anchorage. With considerably more business acumen than I ever had, she stayed at it longer and made a lot more money. Though we now live on the opposite sides of the country and see each other infrequently, our bond remains. As health problems entered our lives, we reconnected more often. One day, a box of two dozen red roses arrived from Des. For no particular reason. To make up for all the birthdays and anniversaries she'd missed, she said.

"Here's to friendship!"

Her Closest Friends Were Men

In the 1960s the Far North was more open, less tradition bound than older communities in the contiguous 48 states. People moved in and out on the flow of military reassignments, the search for adventure or fresh starts. It was a place of newcomers, a place to carve a niche based on interests and ambitions. The daughter of Greek immigrants, Despina Chiamis Lester was among the few young Caucasians born in Anchorage. Ever her father's daughter, Des inherited his keen sense of how to run a business and make money on her own. This during a time when women could barely get a credit card or loan without the signature of a husband. Little wonder, perhaps, that as a woman in a man's world she found friendships among men.

"I am probably an odd woman but my closest friends in my lifetime were men," she says. "Not in the romantic sense at all but just plain buddies. I didn't sleep around with any of them although I could have, but our friendships endured for over 40 years because I refused to ruin it all by destroying friendship in order to experience romance probably for a short time. My 'buddies' understood completely. There are three men who have been my very close dear friends for over 50 years and would do anything for me if I asked and I would do anything for them.

"I have several women friends and many female acquaintances. Those women that I consider my real 'friends' I've known for 40 years or more.

"I look primarily in a friend that they deserve my respect. I detest dishonesty of any type whether it be man or woman, personal or business.

"I like intelligent people. Usually the ones I most enjoy are not super loud in voice and action. I enjoy humor to its fullest but mostly like friends that have a quiet sense of humor. One male friend of many years brought me a Christmas card and a very expensive bottle of wine and in the card he wrote 'for the girl who has everything' and enclosed a gift certificate for $50 to McDonald's. He knew very well I would never eat at McDonald's. I invited him and my goddaughter and her girlfriends to meet me at McDonald's and we all had a good time.

"Age has never meant too much to me when choosing long term friendships. My father was quite a bit older than my mother so I learned to appreciate my special friends regardless of age or status.

"One of my female friends of more than 45 years and I took a train trip together and were assigned seating at a booth for four persons. The two of us sat on one side and a middle-aged couple sat facing us. It was a 10-hour trip so we had a chance to become somewhat acquainted with one another. He was a professor of psychology at the University of Texas. At the end of the train ride he said to the two of us 'ladies, whatever you have don't ever lose it.' A couple months later she and I were having dinner at a posh restaurant and in a booth enjoying the evening. At the end of our dinner we were chatting and a gentleman walked up to us and said 'ladies, whatever you have hold on to it.' We both sat there shocked that two strange men would say almost the identical words to us. As I grew older I came to realize fully how lucky we were to have such a lasting friendship.

"I think it is difficult for two women to get along all the time. My lifetime friend of more than 70 years and I speak very freely with one another. We hold nothing back. We get along famously and love our friendship and what it stands for. Nothing could ever stand between us. It is a very rare friendship yet we are almost total opposites in personality and most everything else. One other girlfriend, I have to walk on eggshells—she is so touchy and opinionated and set in her ways but I just ignore it after many years and we are close friends for 50 years. I chuckle at some of her idiot notions but I love her and here again we are as opposite as two humans could be.

"Good true friendships are a lot of give and take for lasting relationships. Perhaps mostly give!

"I get along with women but am I interested? No."

***

KATHY & BRIAN

Can men and women be just friends?

"I truly believe you can," says Kathy Zarczynski.

Kathy grew up with four siblings but was closest to a brother one year older, another just one year younger.

"We were always together; if one of us got in trouble our father blamed all three of us.

"I was comfortable with guys."

In high school her best friend was a guy named Brian.

"You can really open up to a guy. It was just the comfort of it. He knew my deep dark secrets."

He came from a big family and "he just listened. He didn't try to sway you. He didn't tell you what to do.

"I don't have a lot of girlfriends. The girlfriends I have, they're there for a reason."

After marrying and moving 50 miles away Kathy continued to see her best friend periodically, during visits to see her mother. Now with two grown sons, she wonders what paths their friendships will take. She's already seen some shifting in her youngest as his friends follow their own trajectory into marriage and parenthood, and assures him that is a natural pattern.

"Some drift away and that's okay. Friends can go their own way and come together years later and it feels like yesterday was the last time I saw them.

"We kept saying for months we'll have lunch, we'll have lunch," she said to Brian. Then he died unexpectedly.

Regretfully, "we never had that lunch."

Chapter Fourteen

Constantly talking isn't necessarily communicating.
Charlie Kaufman

No Words Needed

I met Mary when she led theater tours to London while theater professor at State University of New York Fredonia. Most participants, like us, were theater enthusiasts well past our college years. After retirement she moved to North Carolina, to Maine, then back to Fredonia. Now she spends days painting. Two of her colorful pieces, my dog Bentley and a raven, hang on my walls. Once a week she teaches me chess, often followed by pizza.

Mary & the Nuns

In 1982, Mary Charbonnet and her mother spent a week and a half on Crete, with Chania as their home base.

"What a wonderful town that was. Gorgeous harbor with very few tourists—this was before Americans discovered that there was an airport there, and travel agents were directing travelers almost exclusively to Heraklion, site of Knossos also known as the Palace of Minos."

They rented a car and explored the island of Crete on their own with a travel book and map. While touring the island they discovered incredible ocean views, gardens and herds of sheep around every curve. Two lane roads, no interstates.

One highlight was finding an ancient monastery and roaming over it at will, with no other tourists in sight.

"It seemed deserted until I ran into Sister Marie, an equally ancient nun, who was out collecting firewood. I was in the act of taking a photo of an adorable little cat sound asleep in a pot of bright red geraniums when the nun appeared with her small plastic bucket of wood tucked into the notch between her upper arm and the inch of lower arm left after an amputation. She smiled, as only a sweet nun can, and indicated that she would be quiet until I had taken my photo.

"When I lowered my camera, I was horrified to witness this lovely, aged woman suddenly hurl a stick of firewood with the accuracy of a professional baseball pitcher, decapitating several geraniums and causing the cat to let out a terrified scream and fly down the road! She shrugged in response to the shocked look on my face, and indicated her indignation, in sign language, that the cat deserved it for destroying her flowers."

Then she invited Mary into the tiny apartment she shared with her even older sister, also a nun. Mary spotted her mom through the one small window, and beckoned for her to join them. The sisters gave them a tour of the two-room apartment they called home, and offered them a few hard candies and their first taste of locally made raki served in a little shot glass.

"Wow! Powerful stuff!"

"Although they spoke no English and we spoke no Greek, we understood one another perfectly and it turned out to be my happiest, and most memorable Crete day."

Chapter Fifteen

Whether it is by coincidence, chance or Divine Providence, a brief meeting can grow to a relationship that enriches life. And in some cases, transform it.

Daisaku Ikeda

Chance Encounters

Looking back on some of our most cherished relationships, it can seem a miracle that they even began. Another few minutes, another day and we might never have met at all, never mind become friends.

Hildegard & Liz

Hildegard Ratliff lives in an active senior complex in Denver, and Monday is her assigned wash day in the communal laundry room. On this day it was also Christmas. As she walked her laundry down the hallway, a woman came out of the laundry room, looked at her, and said "Oh no!"

Hildegard said "I am scheduled to wash at 3 p.m." Liz already had two machines running.

"I am so confused. I don't even know anymore what I am doing," Liz said. She was exhausted. Hildegard knew she worked as a nurse. She hugged Liz and told her it was okay. She had made the same mistake once. Liz had two more loads waiting to wash.

"I went back to my apartment. I was pissed; then I thought 'it's Christmas. That's not loving your neighbor.' I wrote on a Christmas card *Stop by my place for an eggnog* and taped it on the washing machine."

Soon there was a knock on her door, and they toasted with eggnog with brandy. Hildegard learned that Liz had worked that morning and her client had apologized for not having Christmas dinner for her. The client was invited elsewhere.

"My brain kicked in. She has not eaten. I asked her to check the laundry cycle and then come back. During that time I fixed her a plate with my left-overs from Christmas Eve dinner. I had Angus prime rib, mashed potatoes, green beans, shrimp cocktail, home-baked bread. Of course we had another eggnog too."

Hildegard mentioned she was writing a story about friendship for this book and that she was co-author for *Red & Blue*. Liz was fascinated; she wanted to buy the book. Hildegard happened to have a few copies left and in her inimitable way, sold her one. Next day she found a Christmas card under her door, a great big *thank you* and money for the book. "What a great Christmas for both of us, my newly-found friend Liz."

***

Mary & Rita

Mary Simons was flying to Norfolk, Virginia, to see her sister when she had a layover in Atlanta.

She saw a woman approach the airline ticket counter and "the way she carried herself I thought she had a military background." After finishing her discussion with airline personnel she walked over and sat next to Mary.

"I couldn't help ask about the military," Mary says, "and she said she was a Navy nurse." They talked for a while until boarding was announced. On board they discovered they were assigned seats next to each other. They talked all the way to Norfolk. When they got off the plane they exchanged addresses and phone numbers. Her name is Rita Smith.

After a decade they are still good friends. Mary and Rita talk often on the phone, send e-mails and exchange little things that remind them of each other. Mary visited her in Virginia Beach.

"Blessings come in ways unknown! How lucky for me!"

***

For several years I lived across the field from Liz. When she gave up driving in her 90s I started taking her to grocery stores and medical appointments. She surpassed the century mark, still living alone with her cat. After she passed at 103 her home was inherited by her niece, Erin, my new neighbor.

Erin & Erin

Erin Horlacher has been friends with a woman with whom she shares a first name and initial since kindergarten, over four decades.

They met at Christmas time in school. "Santa" (the custodian) left ornaments on their desks while they were out, decorated with students' names in glitter. Erin X got two, and Erin H. got none. The teacher introduced them, and Erin X gave Erin H. her "extra" ornament.

"Even Santa makes mistakes once in a while. It's forgivable," says Erin H. "Anyway, we still refer to each other as Erin One and Erin Two, never certain which one is which."

Their lives took different paths. Erin X stayed closer to home, married and raised a family. Erin H. did none of the three, moving to California from her native New York.

Both are creative and enjoy the arts.

"We both choose to form our own opinions versus following the pack mentality. We are both willing to make decisions other people may not understand, and can bear the weight of the consequences. We know when to stand up to something we feel is wrong. It's not important how we're seen in the moment."

Erin H. chose not to attend her graduation ceremony in protest to issues in their high school experience. Erin X attended, but walked out during the ceremony at a key moment.

"I guess that's a difference and a similarity in how we handled ourselves. I really admire her for that. She demonstrated a lot of self-respect and dignity that night."

Despite years of geographical separation their friendship endures.

"Besides that we imprinted on each other as children. I'd say that having been through a similar experience, and a similar upbringing in close neighborhoods explains a lot of that, but mostly I just have so much respect and affection for her. She is a grade-school educator now. And she has always had kind, supportive, humorous words for me in tough times.

"She made sure to be in touch with supportive words while my father was sick and dying—having been through it herself with her parents—and during that time for her I wasn't really around much, we were out-of-touch then. I went to California and really disappeared for years from everyone."

What leaves her in awe about her friend?

"She is just such a good person."

***

Hildegard & Robin & Me

In mid-October I flew to golden Denver with its bright blue Colorado skies, famously brilliant autumn colors and light jacket temperatures. Though I stayed with Hildegard in her ground floor condo overlooking a golf course, visiting her was not the main reason for my visit.

It was to meet Robin, a 16-year-old high school exchange student from near Köln, Germany. I'd previously known him only through email correspondence after being introduced by Hildegard. He was spending the school year in suburban Indianapolis, IN. With a fall break in classes, he flew to Denver as well.

In our week together we walked a graveyard with every imaginable nationality on tombstones, some in languages we could not even recognize. They likely could not all get along in life, underground they were all equal. We read heart-rending stories of young lives ended, we tried to peer inside grand mausoleums.

We went to Sunday services at the New Apostolic Church with Hildegard. Robin was raised Catholic but has reached the stage of questioning. He wore wooden beads from a Buddhist Temple in Indianapolis and a chain with the Virgin Mary.

At the Denver Art Museum the portrait exhibit transported us all to other levels of consciousness, as museums are meant to do.

We were an unlikely troika, two women old enough to be his grandmother and an engaging teen mature well beyond his years. An old soul, I call him. When he wore his large brown glasses you could be forgiven for mistaking him for Harry Potter.

Hildegard Ratliff and Robin Siminski met by chance when she was over 80 and he was barely in his teens. Each tells about meeting and getting acquainted from their point of view.

Hildegard's Story

As I left he looked up at me and said "can I write to you?"

"Of course you can," I answered.

Robin wanted to improve his English. We only met that afternoon, at my brother's birthday party. Kiona, my brother Manfred's granddaughter, brought Robin, a school friend.

Robin was fascinated. Here was someone, me, from across the pond, a world that he could only imagine and dream about.

What struck me about him: his politeness, he was into writing stories—*The Bucket List* was among them, his imagination and understanding of the soul. The kid was only 13 years old and had a great smile.

We decided to write to each other. I would correct his English. I told him when he gets stuck just keep writing in German, as long as the thought got on paper.

First few letters were a mess but we ploughed through.

Robin got better and better and I introduced him to my friend Judy through email. Judy and I had worked in Alaska; we each had our own tour business. Over the years we compiled our notes; we wrote a book together about our experiences with travelers. Thus *Red & Blue* was born.

I had taken a copy with me on my visit to Germany. Not everyone in my family speaks English. Robin got ahold of it and enjoyed it very much. He read what he could.

Judy, the journalist, gave him some good pointers. He became so advanced in English that he started correcting me.

We talked about Robin looking into foreign exchange student programs. He did, studied harder, passed all tests, and was on his way to Indianapolis to a host family in July 2017. He started school in August and on his first break, came to visit me in Denver. Judy came also from New York on the same day.

My neighbor Ned and I picked Robin up from the airport. I told Ned I wonder what he looks like; he is now almost a man. I knew I would remember that smile. He walked past us, turned his head and smiled.

Robin arrived early in the morning. Judy's flight didn't come in until midnight. First things first. He was hungry. We went to Denny's where I had discussed the menu with a waitress prior to his visit. Robin is a vegetarian and had a great meal. He said "it's great to speak German again."

That evening was a dance in the complex where I lived, so Robin and I went to the dance, danced one time and observed some of the seniors. We had to kill time until Judy's arrival. It was a long night. We ate pizza.

They both went to church with me, joined in a chorus rehearsal for a holiday concert in my complex. We took the rail into downtown Denver, had lunch, visited the Denver Art Museum. It was the same museum, albeit smaller, where I worked as a security guard many decades ago. We went to the IMAX show, *Incredible Predators,* at the Denver Museum of

Nature & Science. One day we Skyped with his parents in Kürten and a Juneau friend now living in Paris.

One afternoon when I was worn out, Robin and Judy prepared dinner. They baked stuffed mushrooms I'd bought at a grocery store and made up a picture-perfect green salad while I lay down. That night Judy mixed ingredients for artisan bread which she insisted was the easiest ever. No kneading, no rising other than leaving it on the counter overnight, from 8 to 24 hours. We loved it. Now I make it regularly and Robin makes it for his host family in Indianapolis. Perhaps he will also make it back home.

I planned a celebration of Judy's September birthday and Rob's in November with family and neighbors, telling each the party was for the other. I kept it from Rob who was genuinely surprised at a cake with his name as well; Judy and I've known each too long to fool each other. And I needed her help to pick up the cake at the grocery store and keep Rob occupied outside while I spirited the cake into my bedroom.

On his last day, after Judy had returned to New York, neighbors drove Robin and me into the mountains on a sunny golden day. He was totally captivated, as he was from his first day.

Robin, Rob is what we call him now, is still in love with Colorado. It's not "California Dreaming," he says with nod to the popular song, it's "Colorado dreaming."

His visit was the highlight of my year.

Hildegard's poem about our time together in Denver

A frazzled toothbrush
Wet towels
Empty water bottle
Hairs in sink.
We learned from each other
Exchanged many views
Didn't have time to catch the news.
Museum, art gallery a must.
Church and choir
We sang and danced
Skyped and baked bread
Had a great time before we sent the *kid* back.

My No-Knead Crusty Artisan Bread Traveling Around the World

Ingredients
3 cups all-purpose flour
2 t. kosher salt (not table salt)
1 t. active dry yeast
1 ½ cups lukewarm water.

Directions
In a large bowl stir together the flour, salt and yeast. Stir in water using a wooden spoon until mixture forms a shaggy but cohesive dough. Do not over-work dough.

Cover bowl tightly with plastic wrap. Let dough sit at room temperature for 8-24 hours. Dough will bubble up and rise.

After dough is ready, preheat oven to 450 degrees F. Place Dutch oven, uncovered, into the preheated oven for 30 minutes. Cast iron skillet can also be used.

While Dutch oven preheats, form dough into a ball with floured hands. Cover dough loosely with plastic wrap and let rest.

When 30 minutes are up, remove Dutch oven. With floured hands place bread dough inside.

Cover and bake for 30 minutes. Remove cover and bake about 15 minutes more.

Remove to cutting board or wire rack to cool.

Notes
Use one cup of whole wheat flour for denser bread.
No need to grease Dutch oven.
Use any large oven-safe dish. Cover with aluminum foil in lieu of cover.
Herbs, spices, chopped nuts, cheese can be added to dry flour mix before adding water.

Robin's Story

Saturday night, October 2013.

After watching *The Heat* with Melissa McCarthy and Sandra Bullock, Kiona (my school friend) and I both went to bed.

How is she? What will we talk about?

What will I ask her?

The next morning, Sunday. A gray day. I remember that I put on my suspenders and after that we were all excited for her to come.

There she was, standing in the open doorway with a big smile and even bigger glasses. She embraced everyone and said something in a specific German dialect to me. I knew immediately where in Germany she was raised.

We had a wonderful lunch together. Afterwards we had some good conversations about everything and anything. And of course she had some good stories to tell.

We sat a little bit outside and had a delicious desert. We all decided to take a walk to the horses so we did. As we were walking the gray sky converted into a blue sky with a few clouds and the evening sun.

Once we came back and Hildegard was about to leave, I asked her if I could write letters to her to improve my English. And she said yes, of course and gave me a card with her address and another woman's address who turned out also to be a part of my life. Now as I write these lines down I remember how nervous I was to ask her that question

Hildegard pulled out her notebook and I wrote her address. Subsequently she had to go and she gave us all a warm hug and a kiss on our cheeks. I felt so welcomed and embraced in her presence.

I remember how I wrote my first letter to her after she returned to the United States. It was a short letter and the paper color was blue, like her nickname, and I now notice I wrote about random things like what grades I had achieved in my classes at school. And finally sent it out. When I read my first letter today I really can say that my English has improved.

It was Monday and I came home from school. It must have been around November because it was already dark outside. I checked the mailbox and there it was. A letter with the letters USA. I went back inside and opened it with my mother. In it were postcards from the Rocky Mountains, all full of Hildegard's cursive handwriting. Attached to the card was one $5 bill that I kept until I went to the U.S.

My mother helped me read the letter while I was sitting in her lap. She wrote about her beginnings in the United States and corrected my letter. So I wrote a new letter and that went on and on.

Over the next few months, or I should better say over the next year, I received and wrote letters regularly. I showed them to people who are important to me and asked them if they could help me translate them.

After a suitcase of letters and a whole year I had not only improved my English, I had found a friend on the other side of the Atlantic. Something special and rare. I could finally let go and write about anything and after two weeks you got a response with lovely advice or story of Hildegard's life. Like a magical diary when you can let go of all your thoughts and it talks back to you. Even if we had only met for a couple of hours we had created a friendship.

One Friday before the beginning of my Easter break 2014 I took a test in science and sat next to one of my classmates, Fynn. I barely remember that he asked me for an eraser. The next day I found myself sitting next to my aunt in a plane on its way to London. Incidentally I met Fynn's English and sports teacher on that plane. We greeted each other and enjoyed our short flight into the gray, cloudy but gorgeous city of London.

My aunt and I had some great days in England's capital. But on Monday when we came back to our hotel I got 100 messages on my cellphone. Everyone was talking about Fynn and that he passed away. At first I thought it was a joke. But it wasn't. I wasn't really close to him. I just knew him because we had some classes together. But even that was hard to realize that a person doesn't walk, think, doesn't exist anymore is very difficult.

I wrote to Hildegard about it and I received a wonderful letter and a little glass dove in the envelope which I still have. This letter was signed with the words "Your Adopted Grandma." These last words just made me very happy and meant a lot to me.

As our friendship got closer my interest in the United States got bigger. I decided to apply for an exchange year, actually a scholarship from the German government that would cover all the costs. My English teachers at the time gave me a flier attached with an application. I asked my parents and they said yes. I did everything they told me to do and I finally had a group interview. After that each one of us had a separate meeting with one of the congressmen. They chose another boy who I knew through the program. But I decided to try again the following year and I made it.

Now I am sitting here, drinking the hot chocolate that Hildegard sent me for Christmas. The last days of 2017 we took a walk and are now warming up inside the house with John Lennon in my ears. I think back to the beautiful five months I had, mostly in Greenfield, Indiana.

I remember the wonderful week I had in Denver, Colorado. I really had the chance to meet my adopted grandmother again and Judy for the first time. We had great conversations and good food. We saw a lot of things and learned a lot of things we didn't know from each other.

Judy Shuler

Robin's Poem About His Year as an Exchange Student

Where I'm From

I'm from my grandma's
gardening hand.
I'm from a place where
potatoes and rosebuds still
blossom.

I'm from the woods and
the creeks.
I'm from cowpats and
barns.
I'm from summer and
winter.

I am from cornfields
and lush green hills.
I am from rumpled
drawings,
the costumes in the
basement
and the stories that they
tell.

I'm from my mother's
…..smell
I'm from my dad's
tender cross sign on
my forehead.
Am I from love?

I'm from Germany,
that's where I'm from.

I'm living in the States.
When I go back,
where am I from?

It depends on where we go,
to tell where we are from.
I am going back,
back to where I am from
or better
where I was from.

***

I met Jerry and Sandy in the couple's club of First United Methodist Church in Anchorage where Fred and I were married the previous year.

JERRY & SANDY & MARTIN

Three days led to friendship spanning a lifetime.

Servas International seeks to build world peace, goodwill and understanding by bringing together people of different cultures, backgrounds and nationalities. Servas hosts welcome travelers to share their daily lives, typically for two days. It is hoped that over a friendly meal or a cup of coffee both may come to understand each other on a deeper level.

In other words, move toward world peace one friendship at a time.

Jerry and Sandy Moore became part of that movement in ways they had not anticipated. They met in a Presbyterian-sponsored singles' group in Southern California, she from the Black Hills of South Dakota, he from rural central Indiana. They married there and in 1970 moved to Anchorage, Alaska, which would remain their home for the next 36 years.

Anchorage was the most open and welcoming of places. Meeting someone and inviting them home for dinner was a common occurrence. Jerry and Sandy fit right into that culture.

Jerry's sister, a host member of SERVAS also lived in Anchorage. Unable to host when she was expecting her second child, she asked Jerry and Sandy to step in. It was 1984 and they agreed to open their home to a single young school teacher, Martin Davies, from Wales, U.K.

"He was a delightful house guest, just ending an extensive summer road trip throughout Alaska, but had a dilemma. He needed a buyer for his vehicle. Funds would pay airfare to Los Angeles, where he would connect to London via his round trip return ticket," Sandy says.

"On a beautiful Labor Day weekend no one had responded to his newspaper ad, so we did. Jerry bought his airline ticket in exchange for the car title, and we waved him off. We sold the vehicle (for the amount of the airfare—maybe a bargain?) to the first person who answered our ad.

"Martin, an educator now married and retired, a world traveler, and all-around great guy has been a faithful correspondent since then—travel postcards and annual Christmas greetings."

Sandy and Jerry now live in Indiana, closer to Jerry's family and about three hours from Chicago's O'Hare International Airport.

They've had three visits from Martin and his wife Helen as they began or ended road trips through the Lower 48 states. He has visited all 50 states, many more than once. Helen has met some of his life-long friends all over the U.S.

"Once, he mentioned the name of a Wyoming couple they would see. Surprise, surprise—it was a couple we had met years earlier in the Anchorage home of good friends. One year we were in Wyoming for a family visit at the same time Martin and Helen were in the area, so a breakfast meeting was arranged; they were on their way to visit their Wyoming friend, a former Servas host, who is now a good friend of ours."

All because Jerry stepped in for his sister and answered their own house guest's ad: car for sale.

Sandy says the secret for sustaining and nurturing friendship includes faithful correspondence, sincere curiosity—asking and listening—and a desire to stay connected through shared interests. Enriched by opportunities for personal visits.

"Friendships are one of the best of life's blessings, and ours are treasured, as we often tell our friends."

A magnet on their refrigerator, gift from a houseguest, speaks volumes.

"Good friends are hard to find, difficult to leave, and impossible to forget."

Chapter Sixteen

Each friend represents a world in us, a world possibly not born until they arrive, and it is only by this meeting that a new world is born.
Anaïs Nin

Friends Who Save Us

There are friends for coffee and conversation, for going to movies or concerts, for shopping yard sales. Then there are friends who change our lives.

I met Mickey and Lori through Hildegard, who once lived across the street from them. It would be decades before I learned the whole of their story.

MICKEY & LORI

With a homemade wooden camper over the bed and cab of her Ford Econoline pick-up truck, Mickey Leslie headed north. In the rear view mirror, the state of Kansas where she grew up and returned to build the camper with the help of a friend, and her recent home and job in Michigan. Ahead lay the 1,500-mile Alcan, now called the Alaska Highway.

Spurred by World War II, the Alcan was constructed in nine months during 1942 to offer land access for equipment and supplies between the contiguous United States and then Territory of Alaska. It was June, 1965, when she set out. The Alcan was still mainly gravel through Canada and barely paved in Alaska, infamous for cracked windshields and headlights, flat tires and busted axels. And for miles between service stations. A coat of mud was telltale sign of any vehicle driving the road. It was quite an undertaking for a woman alone in her early 30s.

Before embarking on her trip she met a couple from Palmer, Alaska, who warned her not to drive over 45 miles per hour to avoid flat tires from shale on the highway and to lessen the chance of broken windshield. The upper window of her camper was eventually broken. She taped cardboard over it and bought plastic bubbles for the headlights. By Watson Lake, Yukon Territory, she'd lost an overload spring, grounding her in a campground for a week until a replacement could arrive by bus from Edmonton, Alberta.

All along the Alcan campgrounds were sited on a lake or river. Each night she washed off the truck. It was before power steering and "my shoulders were tight as a drum by evening," she says. "This loosened them up."

Mickey was bent on getting as far as possible from the life she left behind.

She continued on into Alaska, turning north to Fairbanks, then driving south to Anchorage. Just over a year had passed since the 1964 Good Friday Alaskan earthquake, largest to ever hit North America, and widespread damage remained.

She naively asked at an Anchorage gas station why Fourth Avenue had such large parking lots with no visible businesses nearby. "Earthquake of course."

The people from Palmer she'd met in Kansas were back home by then. When she stopped by for a visit, they took her along on a drive to the coastal town of Seward. "I was astounded and overwhelmed," she remembers. "I'd seen lots of tornado damage all my life, but it didn't compare to seeing the waterfront in Seward. Huge slabs of concrete broken and jumbled up like river ice break up."

Both Anchorage and Fairbanks were too big, she decided. So she drove back down the highway through the Yukon Territory and Northern British Columbia to the Alaska port city of Haines. Nearly at the end of the trip she got the dreaded cracked windshield. But never a flat tire. In Haines she drove her camper onto a ferry of the Alaska Marine Highway, connecting communities along the Inside Passage with no road link.

Four and one-half hours later she disembarked in Juneau, Alaska's capital city.

"When I got off in Juneau—I'd never seen anything like it or knew it existed. This was the place."

From the flat lands of Kansas and Michigan Mickey came into downtown Juneau, where mountain and beach are sometimes less than a block apart. Mountains climb from sea level to 3,500 feet, covered with dense spruce and hemlock forest until tree-line, where summer alpine slopes are covered with ground-hugging blueberries, salmonberries, dwarf dogwood. In winter they're buried by a hundred feet of snow and battered by winds that would qualify as Level 4 hurricanes on the Atlantic coast. And it met her criteria for a small town, then only 14,000 people.

Mickey grew up in an orphanage in rural Kansas. Her dad died of pneumonia in 1935 when she was one year old. It would be another seven years before penicillin might have saved him. At the time her widowed mother's employment options were housekeeper, teacher, or nurse, living in a room in someone else's house. From the age of two Mickey was moved to an orphanage with her brother, four, and sister, six. To visit her children, Mickey's mother had to take a bus, get off on the highway, and walk one and one-half miles down a dirt road to reach the home. Then she had to walk back and wait for a bus to town. Five years later her mother also died.

"We probably saw her three or four times before she died," Mickey says. "I had no idea who she was or what a mother was. A parent or close relative had to take you out—they didn't adopt. So I spent 16 years in that place."

The home was not only geographically isolated, but socially removed from everyday lessons most children learn in their families. "We knew no social graces or how to mix," she says.

She recalls getting off the property only once. "We kids (36) were loaned to the Eisenhower farm in Abilene, 46 miles away, to get the watermelons in before a hail storm. The General was home on leave and we met him. He loved us little ones—I was the smallest."

Caroline, who worked as a seamstress in the orphanage, became a nurturing life-long friend. "All our clothes were made—inside out, top to bottom—though I had hand-me-downs to age 14,"she says

They were both "a little bit like lost souls," Mickey says. "She wasn't a mother substitute, but a gentle mentor for the remainder of her life."

"A steadying influence," Mickey calls her.

Caroline had a mid-life baby boy "and he became my boy, on my shoulders as much as possible."

"My other outlet was Jerry the old one-eyed mule. When all failed or I had one whipping too many, I'd stand in his trough and hug his neck and cry. Never did get big enough to reach all way around his neck. And he probably slept through the whole thing!! Never moved!"

Eventually the orphanage closed its school when the numbers dropped from 90 students to about 60. "And off to town we were bussed. We weren't treated kindly by the other kids."

Caroline helped Mickey understand "how different we were from the town kids," though she didn't know what the town kids thought of the orphanage. Not until Mickey went to her 35th high school reunion did she learn that other students thought the place was a reformatory. "They thought we were there because we'd done something bad."

Mickey went straight from the home into the U.S. Air Force for five years. When all the children left the orphanage at 18 "we knew nothing about how to get along. Not that one needed an application for a job and an apartment. Where and how to find one. Girls in the Air Force had to take me into town and show me how to purchase socks and underwear. I didn't see the inside of a house until after the Air Force at age 24."

"I knew only how to help cook for 150 people, drive tractor, mow alfalfa and rake it, throw 70-pound bales of hay on a wagon, since age 13. Milk 60 head of cattle at 4 a.m. with brother and one other boy. Weld machinery when something broke and wait tables (4-6 people each) for old folks before school and after.

"In basic training my flight unit had two gals from New York City. They were probably 20 or 21, real old to us 18ers. One night walking by the Drill Instructor room I heard her tell them 'if you want to get along, play ball.' So after basic, at my first station, I played basketball, softball, volleyball, handball. It was three years before I knew what she meant."

Through it all Caroline's guidance was "essential for years and she freely gave it. She knew how much to help and when to make me learn on my own."

Mickey says it was during her third year in the Air Force that she realized she was gay. "But it was also when I learned it had better be the deepest darkest secret you ever had. You would receive a dishonorable discharge for being gay.

"You couldn't be seen speaking to anyone living in town who had been discharged or anyone on base awaiting discharge. You would be dishonorably discharged for 'association.'

"You were under suspicion if you wore a tailored shirt and you could be questioned for days—'are you gay?'—by a 6-foot man lording over you.

"In the 50s women didn't wear shirts. They wore blouses. Since I didn't know what a tailored shirt was I stayed in uniform at all times. From overhearing conversations I learned that federal law criminalized homosexuality. We're talking federal prison here.

"At year five of my military career I was stationed where we had rooms of three people instead of two-story open bay barracks of 50 women each. We got along although one gal was kinda quirky. One day my other roommate went to the room at noon and found her on her bunk with her wrists slit.

"She survived but I was immediately called in by the OSI (Office of Special Investigations) and grilled. They insisted she was in love with me. Other than refusing their accusations I didn't know how to defend myself and fervently wished my brother was an attorney instead of an astrophysicist with his head in the clouds.

"At the time the Air Force was going through a period of 'if you don't intend to re-enlist you can get out six months early.'

"It was two days before Christmas and no one ever pushed a discharge through as quickly as I did running from building to building for signatures. The OSI office was closed for the holiday so there was no one to 'red line' me and stop my discharge."

After returning to civilian life, Mickey worked 10 years on an Army base as cryptologist, the same work she had done in the Air Force.

"Now all that could happen is lose my apartment, job and federal pension. Since my work was with a top secret clearance I had two ways to go to a federal pen."

As a woman and only single person she was designated to work the night shift. "No social life. No trouble," she thought.

Days she went to college. "If you changed your major every couple years, you could go for one degree while doing master's for the previous one. I guarantee it keeps you off the streets, out of trouble. Getting smarter is questionable."

"Finally deciding I needed a change I transferred to Michigan. There I met a gal named Loraine Rueff.

"She fell head over heels for me while hardly knowing me. I couldn't see any way out of this so I packed up my truck and fled to Alaska! After corresponding for eight months she showed up on my doorstep." Three years later Lori too moved north.

"Then we discovered you could get chased out of state with blue cards, a one-way ticket out of Alaska for undesirables. Not lose your apartment and job—run out of the state!" In Alaska homosexuality was not fully decriminalized until 1980.

"She was a bit older (14 years) than me with prematurely frosted hair. One couple who lived near even thought she was my mother. That seemed a good cover. We never knew but one other gay couple in our 45 years together."

They shared a love of words—"read a word and end up with six *Encyclopedia Britannica* on the floor as one word leads to another." They read non-fiction and history, wrote, hiked in the Yukon together for 28 years. Eventually Mickey compiled stories and photos of their adventures into an illustrated book, *Exploring Alaska and Western Canada with Mickey Lesley and Friends*. Copies are available from the author at P.O. Box 32739, Juneau, AK 99803.

"Our spirits bonded and we did so much of the same—vast correspondence, reading, being homebodies.

"But we weren't wedded at the hip. She went to drinking lunches with newspaper friends and I went to dinners with my State of Alaska Department of Fish & Game guys, fellow agency employees."

Lori was a big city girl who knew nothing about farms or animals. Mickey knew nothing of big city life except "it's scary." Lori was full German who grew up with grandparents following strict old ways. Mickey was all Irish.

Lori "knew all about authors and classical music. At my age 41 she introduced me to *Wind in the Willows* and nursery rhymes I'd never heard of."

Despite the challenges, Mickey says her relationship with Lori lasted "because she fell in love with me and there was no way she was going to let me get away. I had never thought about love, probably because I never expected anyone to love me.

"She made my life worth something and complete."

Lori was "the only intellectual I ever knowingly knew. Her head was a computer…before computers."

Caroline remained a nurturing friend to Mickey until her death at the age of 96.

"She was so proud when I loaded my truck and headed for Alaska and love found me in my early 30s. She even loved my being gay. What better friend can you have? Her son is still my little brother and we're close." Caroline visited Mickey in Alaska twice; her son also visits Mickey.

Eventually Lori's health gradually declined.

"At first she gave up driving and would go on errands with me. Then she would go, but not get of out of the car. Then it was too much trouble getting in and out of the car so she stayed home. Then she could fix breakfast and lunch but not dinner—and one at a time they went, then serious caregiving."

When Mickey got thyroid cancer three doctors told her it was from stress. During an annual eye exam she had a seizure in the ophthalmologist's office. Again she was told it was due to stress. It was time to move Lori into a state-owned Pioneer Home for care.

"Two members of the staff declared they were gay—right out in the open! It scared the wits out of us.

"Loraine is gone now. I wish she could have seen the change in society and perhaps joined Juneau's gay community. Even though all of the states only recently no longer have the criminalization law, it is still hard to let go after a lifetime of fear and hiding."

Three years after Lori's passing, Mickey told her story at *The Mudrooms*, a monthly program where everyday people tell their real life stories. On this night the theme for all seven speakers was "Letting Go." Word of her participation appeared in advance on Facebook, and in the packed venue the closest chair was just six feet away from her.

"I knew it was a powerful presentation but I only took one step back from the microphone and the place erupted, and it went on and on. I was told by the program director that in the six years of the program that's the only standing ovation they have ever had."

During a break in the program "I no more than got to my feet than I was mobbed and a long line waiting. Half of them had tears in their eyes. Two women who had gay sons and no idea of the uneducated prejudice that still exists.

"Many 'thank you' and 'how brave of you.' It made me realize people are still afraid to come out of the closet. When the 15 minutes was over I was exhausted. Even some men came with hugs—as did everyone.

"And Lori had the best seat in the house!

"I'm not here to let go of the grief and sadness of losing Lori," she told the audience. "No, I'm here letting go of a lifetime of fear and hiding.

"We had 45 wonderful years together while hiding in our own cocoon," Mickey says.

"The day she died she told me 'it' was right with God. I'm still awed that she could love me like that for 45 years."

***

I learned about Judy and her story of friendship through a mutual friend.

JUDY & JUNE

In 1968 Judy Singer was a nun in a Dominican convent in Belen, New Mexico. She taught first grade in a Catholic school.

Members of the religious community met occasionally to talk about pertinent matters in small groups. When it was time for each table to report on their discussion to the whole group Judy was too shy, too fearful and anxious to speak up.

That fall four people came from Albuquerque to lead a workshop designed to help people listen and speak their truth. Attendees came from other denominations as well. They were all sitting in a classroom before sessions began when June Stevens, one of the facilitators, walked in the door.

June's eyes met Judy's and "something happened," Judy says. They were divided into two groups and Judy kept hoping she would be in June's group. She was. A man named Ray led the group. At close of the session he announced they would meet again the next day and they needed a discussion leader.

Participants kept nominating each other to be leader; Ray kept insisting the person must volunteer themselves. After what seemed like an interminable length of time to Judy, "finally, I don't know what possessed me, I said 'I'll do it.' "

During the meeting June had recorded who spoke and how much. She made the point that when you're in a group, everyone is responsible for sharing.

"Don't worry," June told Judy afterwards. "It will all be fine. Everyone is in charge."

The next day her group of two dozen had shrunk by more than half. Serving as group leader went okay, Judy says, because she had eye contact with June and that gave her confidence. Moreover, Judy ended up moderator for the entire workshop. When it concluded June invited participants to a party at her house in Albuquerque, 35 miles away.

At the end of the party June told Judy "If you come to Albuquerque, come for a visit."

One of the women in her convent had a weekly appointment in Albuquerque. Since nuns went out two by two at that time, Judy rode along and every Thursday she and June would have a couple of hours together.

"We talked non-stop."

June was a Presbyterian minister's wife trying to figure out who she was apart from that role, Judy was trying to figure out who she was apart from being a nun. They read psychology, philosophy, self-help books and discussed them in depth.

The people who lived with Judy told her "we can always tell when you were with June because your eyes sparkle." June was about the age of Judy's mother, but treated her as a sister.

The following spring, when it was time for assignments at the convent, Judy was asked if she wanted to stay or move.

"Of course I wanted to stay. I'd just met June."

But she was transferred back to her home state of Michigan where she moved into an experimental house with four other nuns in a racially mixed neighborhood. Judy and June wrote to each other, pages and pages. They were of a whole different quality, she says, with a deeper sharing than usually found in letters.

June came to see her, and invited Judy to visit her in Albuquerque again. June would pay for travel. Judy went to the Mother House for permission and was told "no."

After a few more years Judy felt maybe she didn't belong in a convent, and went into group therapy for a short time. When a woman who'd left the convent sent back a photo with her husband and adopted bi-racial children, Judy thought "how lucky." She identified most with the lay people in her group but when it was over she said she'd stay in the convent.

Shortly after, she went out to visit June and her husband Paul–this time she didn't ask permission first. The first few days of her visit Judy was filled with confidence. Then June noticed Judy was wearing a ring, which she hadn't done in New Mexico.

"Can you tell me about it?" June asked.

"It's a sign of my commitment to Christ."

"Does it mean more? Do you want to be married?"

"I got so afraid I couldn't even answer."

"Whenever I ask you a question and you don't want to answer, you don't have to," June told her. "But maybe it's a question you have to answer for yourself."

After that, her confidence shattered, Judy could not answer the most basic questions. What she wanted for breakfast.

Whether she'd like Paul to drive her to Santa Fe to see July Fourth fireworks. Judy was beside herself.

"I'm thinking I'd like to leave the convent but I don't know how." She didn't know how to get an apartment, get a car, get a job. Yet she had done all these things prior to entering the convent.

Later she'd say to June, "I think I will leave the convent. I think you'd like me to do that."

June replied, "If you'd like to leave the convent I will support you. If you want to stay I will support you. It doesn't matter to me. I will love you either way."

Judy came to tears. "That's what God's love must be like," she thought. She'd never before felt that unconditional love. She felt walls crumbling around her, the floor falling away. "But because of her love for me it didn't frighten me. It was energizing."

As a child Judy thought she wanted to marry and have 13 children. Yet she graduated high school and went through two years of college without a real date. Part of her thought no one would ever want to marry her. While in college she attended Mass daily. She argued with God, but had a feeling He wanted her in a convent. She opened Thomas à Kempis looking for answers. A Dominican priest she really liked befriended her, and partly because of that she entered a convent, perhaps unconsciously to impress him.

After she returned from her visit with June and Paul, she went on a retreat with classmates, then back to her experimental house. She taught one more year, spending a good part of that year in therapy with a Presbyterian minister who lived across the street. When the year was over, she'd made the decision to leave. Her confidence had returned. When she went to the Mother House, they didn't even question her decision or try to persuade her to stay.

Judy and June continued corresponding, then in later years phoning each other. After leaving the convent Judy continued teaching first grade in Catholic school for seven years. And eventually she had the family, husband and son, she had thought was out of reach. All three visited June in Albuquerque. Judy was there for her 90th birthday.

"Of all the people in my life she had the most influence. I feel she helped me wake up. There was just a vast difference after I met her."

***

Hildegard & Michi

Darkness had set in. A few moments earlier, some light was still visible through the small, curtainless window.

"Give me another beer," said the lonely figure.

Hildegard was tending bar. "What's your name?" she asked.

"Merle." Stopping by the bar on his way home was his daily routine. "Just checked my mail—nothing but bills."

Snow started falling over Douglas Island. The window was now a dark spot in the wall with only snowflakes dancing against it. It seemed as if the wind had picked up. Winter had come.

"Hope it's not one of those Taku Winds," Merle said. Hildegard carried on with her work, asking him the usual "are you married?"

"Yeah," he said, "but my wife is an invalid. She's been bedridden for several years with multiple sclerosis. She was a professional musician in her early twenties and played in a band in Eugene, Oregon. That's where we met. We used to have a lot of fun together."

"Can she sit up?" Hildegard asked.

"Yeah," Merle answered.

"Well, what's wrong with putting her in your car and bringing her in, so I can meet her?"

"Never thought of that," Merle replied. He took a few more sips of beer, set down the glass and left.

Old western songs ground away on the juke box as more customers entered the bar. They were glad to be out of the weather, which by now had gotten worse. A trash can blew across the street, spilling its contents into its path. People were holding on to parked cars to keep from sliding. The snow was falling sideways now, guided by the increasing winds.

A loud thud. Everyone stopped and looked toward the door, which was flung open. In came a walker. Hanging on it was a brunette, a woman in her early 40s, dressed in a beige wool suit. Neither Hildegard nor the patrons could believe what they saw.

"Hi," she said. "My name is Michi. Someone asked about me. I had to see for myself who that person was, so here I am."

She had Merle produce a guitar out of the car and asked if she could play in the bar. Old country westerns were her favorite, she remembered them by heart. Before long everyone joined her in singing. She played long past closing time. The winds had calmed down. Snow was falling softly as everyone left.

Hildegard became good friends with Michi and Merle over the years. Michi was struck with the illness, for which there is no cure, in her late 20s, and suffered from various symptoms which drained her strength. The joy of being among people, and the satisfaction of sharing her music with friends, gave her the initiative and the courage to enjoy life again. There was a visible difference. Michi's health improved because now she worked hard to build up herself. She was able to perform light chores around the house, like planning a meal, caring for her plants, and dusting. And playing her music.

Two years after she had come into the bar, Hildegard stopped by one day for a visit. Michi opened her door and walked across the room without aid. As she turned she smiled and said "you did this to me because you had faith in me, you invited me, you cared."

The bartender, Hildegard Ratliff, took no credit but felt she had witnessed a miracle. Michi did not know that Hildegard had kept her in her prayers.

"God has wonderful ways of showing us His love."

***

We are all interwoven in a many-hued tapestry. Through Judy Singer I met Jeff and learned his story of transforming friendship.

JEFF & JUDY & ANDREW & JANEY

"Unconditional love" felt a bit too clichéd; unconditional caring was better, perhaps. By whatever name, Jeffrey W. Barr believes that without it he would now be dead.

He was born one of twins in 1954 in Stow, OH, where his father settled after serving in World War II.

As it does so often, Jeff's father looms large in his life story. He was an engineer for NASA, working on rocket entrance and exit technology. His face was on the cover of *Weekly Reader*, a classroom magazine, when Jeff was a sixth grader.

It was probably about the time of Jeff's birth that a tumor began growing in his father's brain. But it wouldn't be diagnosed for 30 years, when it had grown large as an orange. He became more introverted as he aged, Jeff remembers. Yet he became a different, more outgoing person while singing in various church choirs with his exceptional tenor voice. For young Jeff it was a confusing whiplash, moving weekly between services worshipping a loving God or a jealous God or a vengeful God.

When Jeff was 11 his father's work transferred him to the West Coast. He never returned home. Deeply hurt, his mother turned to alcohol for solace. So did Jeff and his twin sister.

By the time he was 14 Jeff knew he had to escape a toxic household. He enrolled in boarding school and like his father, never went back home

On school vacations he went to other people's homes. He joined Boy Scouts, where he found surrogate fathers. Too young to rent an apartment, he nonetheless got his own place as a high school senior when his father paid the rent in lieu of alimony.

His grandparents financed his first year of college, at a small church-sponsored rural school with no discernable majors. Jeff was too young to know what he wanted, except that that wasn't it. He admittedly majored in extra-curricular activities and dropped out at the end of the year. About the same time he was exposed to Quakerism through his aunt when both participated in peace rallies at Kent State University.

After working four years, older and more mature, he was able to pay his own way into Ohio University, Athens. The straight A's he earned the first semester, plus volunteer work in the interim, garnered full scholarships and housing stipends. Basically a free ride, he says. He pursued a double major, earning undergraduate degrees in health and science education and in recreation studies and outdoor education. At the end of the school term he chanced upon a poster for a meeting that night on international jobs. It offered a choice between Haiti and Colombia. Thinking poverty in Haiti would be overwhelming, he chose Cali, Colombia.

Situated near the equator in the Cauca Valley, at an elevation above 3,000 feet, Cali's surroundings supported rich and varied agriculture, and his first exposure to organic farming. Jeff also met his wife Alice, an expatriate from Maine.

They taught at the leading college preparatory school in Cali. Students largely came from wealthy families, some of them international residents like himself. Others, he would later learn, were children of the drug cartel. One day a guerilla group, M-19, surrounded the school intent on kidnapping students for ransom. It was the cartel who knew they were coming and alerted police. The government army responded with helicopters and blazing machine guns, thwarting the attempt. After it was over, Jeff and his wife decided it was good time to leave.

From Colombia they went to Mogadishu in Somalia in 1989. They were evacuated the following year during overthrow of President Mohamed Siad Barre. While they got out alive, some of their friends did not. Their next location, Bangladesh. She started a computer program for students. He eventually earned a doctorate degree for a rural health education program he developed that addressed life-threatening dehydration.

In 1998, after 13 years abroad, they returned to the United States. His wife was from Kennebunkport, he was from Ohio. "Ohio or Maine? Easy choice." They settled in a 200-year-old New England house. She continued her focus on technology for students when then-Governor Angus King was committed to putting a laptop in the hands of every middle school student. Jeff moved deeper into organic gardening and wanted to move to Chautauqua County, NY, to land previously owned by his late father. She didn't. They separated, then divorced as friends on different paths.

The land was originally acquired sight-unseen through barter. A Navy pilot in the war, Jeff's father bought an unused landing craft at war's end and lived on it in the New York harbor. He couldn't find a buyer after accepting a job offer in Ohio and ended up trading with a U.S. diplomat newly assigned to Haiti, the boat for land.

After retirement, his father at last summered on the land he got in trade. In Fredonia he met his third wife, who was a founding member of Unitarian Universalist Church there. When Jeff visited his father he also visited that church. Ownership passed to Jeff when he completed installment payments and purchased the land in 1994 while still teaching overseas. After his divorce, Jeff moved from Kennebunkport to Chautauqua County.

When he initially arrived Jeff thought he could get a job teaching. First he would have to be certified by the State of New York. His 30 years of teaching and doctoral degree would put him up to $100,000 annual salary under union scale. And he was less than 10 years from retiring himself.

No one would hire him, he was told. "Don't bother."

Unemployed, without friends who had been part of his life around the world, Jeff says he got deeply depressed and turned even more to alcohol, which was never far from his life through the years.

"I became an alcoholic, and probably always was."

About a year after moving to New York he had a diabetic black-out while driving. Six hours later he woke up in jail. Due to breath with a sweet fruity odor typical of diabetic coma, he was arrested for drunk driving. Ironically, he says he drank every day, but never before driving. He had to wait three to four months for a court hearing, then be prepared with just a two-week notice. The physician who could testify to his diabetic condition at the hearing was in Africa volunteering at a mission hospital, and the court would not accept the word of his physician's assistant.

Jeff lost his driver's license and was fined $3,000. Without a car he couldn't work on his property where he planned to build a house, and he didn't have transportation for a job

Yet he counts his arrest as one of the best things that happened to him. It was at last the needed wake-up call.

"It made me realize I did have a drinking problem."

Enter friends.

One of them was Judy Singer, the former nun.

"If it weren't for Judy and Andrew (Maggitti) & Janey (Wagner) I'd probably be dead," he says.

With no transportation, no job, no way to build the house as he'd planned, neighbors he'd met at the Unitarian Church opened their homes for a place to stay and provided support for changing his life.

He and Andrew now pursue organic gardening at Andrew and Janey's home and other locations in the city. Together they provide food for over 30 families throughout the growing season and sell produce at the Fredonia Farmers' Market.

Judy, who left the convent after years of soul-searching, "walks the talk," he says

"We're sisters and brothers."

Jeff attends local AA meetings and leads when needed, and has returned to the Quaker faith he rediscovered while living in Maine.

"The big thing is simplicity," he says.

"For much of life I was living in the future." In the eyes of his mother, who has since passed, he was second chair, never good enough, never quite measuring up.

The measure of true friendship?

Unconditional caring and support.

"When they ask 'how are you?' they want to know how ARE you? Not just physically, but emotionally, spiritually. The whole thing."

With real friends, "what I have you have. Let's celebrate life."

Chapter Seventeen

Friends are part of the glue that holds life and faith together. Powerful stuff.

Jon Katz

When Family and Friendship Circles Blend

Often men and women each have their own circle of same-sex friends. But sometimes whole families embrace each other in one circle of friendship.

BARBARA & LLOYD & CAROL & BILL

Carol was the girl across the street in suburban Pittsburgh where both lived. She and Barbara walked to school together.

Except when they got mad at each other. Then they walked on opposite sides of the street. When they were both in sixth grade their parents moved, Barbara's to Sugar Grove and Carol's to Irvine. They visited each other during summer breaks. During one summer visit to Irvine, Barbara found Carol and her friends speaking Oppish, a secret code where *op* is added after every consonant and vowels are spoken as in the alphabet. "Hello, how are you today?" becomes "H-opp ell-opp o. H-opp ow ar-opp e y-opp ou t-opp od-opp ay?"

"I had no idea what they were saying," Barbara says. But at the end of her two-week visit, she was speaking it too.

After Barbara graduated from high school she rented a house on Lake Erie from friends for $42. Carol came along for the week-long break

It was one of those weeks that shapes lives. Lloyd Corell's boyhood home was less than a mile away. He and Barbara met along the beach. They would be married for 54 years until his passing. Carol's dry wit was a match for Lloyd's ever-present teasing. After Carol married Bill Parkins all four became fast friends, along with the Corell's two sons and a daughter and the Parkins' adopted son and daughter. Their daughter was born a day before Barbara gave birth to their youngest, a boy.

After sixth grade Barbara and Carol never lived in the same place again. But their friendship endured. Barbara moved to Western New York with Lloyd; Carol lived with her math teacher husband in Newark, DE, and worked as hospital medical technician. By then they'd long stopped walking on opposite sides of the street. Through the years there were shared canoe trips on the Alleghany River, visits to each other's homes. Though Lloyd was more of an outdoors guy, he and Bill shared the same kind of sense of humor.

They exchanged letters over the years; now Barbara wishes she'd kept the letters from Carol who passed of debilitating arthritis that eventually crippled her organs. Letters were discarded while preparing to move to another state for Lloyd's work. The transfer did not go through. Lloyd passed of cancer on Barb's birthday. Now Barbara and Bill keep in touch by email.

Barbara and Carol came from similar backgrounds with hard-working parents. Barbara is shorter than manufactured clothes, ever having to shorten sleeves and pant hems. Her jewelry is petite like her, her short hair a light color that keeps gray at bay. She is most at home in her kitchen, near the window where she watches the bluebird house in summer, hummingbirds sipping nectar, Baltimore orioles scarfing grape jelly. It is still where she passes most days, continuing to cook more than many women after they find themselves alone.

Carol's debilitating arthritis began with gnarled hands in her 30s or 40s but "she didn't let it get her down," Barb says. She passed when it hit her lungs in her early 70s.

Barbara is hard-pressed to explain "how we came to like each other so much." Such is the mystery of friendships that grow day by day and endure.

***

Elsie was a pinochle partner after we started spending summers in New York. Little did I know what role she would one day play in our lives.

ELSIE & RICHARD & DELANA & JOHN

Elsie Gustafson wrote these words for the memorial service of her friend, Delana Gilbert.

"We were friends since our kindergarten days at Brocton Central School with Mrs. Furman. By the time we were in junior high we became closer and both belonged to a sorority. We had pajama parties, stayed on Lake Erie in Greencrest for vacations. I spent many nights at Delana's home because she lived closer to town, where the action was, and the Brocton Diner which was a favorite hangout.

"In high school we enjoyed lunch hours dancing to the juke box, which would be unheard of today. On weekends there was always something going on—pajama parties, roller skating at the fire hall or movies at the Lake Theater. Also time was spent on homework when it could be fitted in.

"Graduation was both exciting and sad. We both got office jobs. Delana in Westfield and myself in Dunkirk. We double dated for several years. After marriage (Delana to John, Elsie to Richard "Gus") we vacationed together and marched in the firemen's parades which were big affairs in those days.

"One vacation I remember most vividly, in 1959 or early 60s I believe, was to Cape Cod. We went out for dinner at the East Bay Lodge which was a very exclusive restaurant on the Cape. We all ordered seafood. Delana had a whole huge lobster on her plate. When she was struggling with it on her plate all of a sudden the lobster flew off her plate and slid across the dining room floor. Of course she was humiliated and embarrassed. The waiter brought her a new serving. We laughed about this for hours later that evening.

"Another fond memory is our many week-end stays at the Gilbert cottage on Bear Lake. We had many large gatherings there with friends and their families. The kids all had fun playing. We enjoyed swimming and, for the brave ones, water skiing. We would start every day with Bloody Marys and the local grocer could not keep up with our demand for tomato juice. We had many delicious meals on the grill.

"As our families grew up we still remained close celebrating birthdays and holidays. We also attended many Buffalo Bills games as we had season tickets. We had snowmobiles too and enjoyed the socialization. It was a plus that we ended up being close neighbors and living across the park from each other.

"I could go on and on about my best friend, who was always kind and considerate. She will certainly be sadly missed and will always remain close to my heart."

***

Steve and Anne are my neighbors and pinochle partners. On summer Saturday mornings Anne and I read the classified ads, then hit the road for one of our favorite pastimes, checking out estate and garage sales.

Anne & Steve & Sylvia & Herkey

Anne and Steve LaVoice met their long-time friends Clayton "Herkey" and Sylvia Smith when they bought the house next door.

Often friendships form between men or between women. Sometimes couples find their best friends in the same place.

They first met when "she just came over," Anne says of Sylvia.

Both had three children, girls the same age, a boy the same age as Anne and Steve's twin boys, and a younger girl.

When the children were young they camped together at Allegany State Park; they took them to Disney World seven times. "We didn't do everything together but you don't have to. We did special things," Steve says. Anne and Sylvia baked cookies together and did crafts through Home Bureau programs. Families shared meals at each other's houses. Sylvia's mother lived with the Smiths. When Anne resigned as teacher's aide and returned to nursing school the grandma next door cared for her children. She took a year-long course to become an LPN, started work at a nearby nursing home a week after graduation, and stayed there 21 years. Sylvia was an outgoing kindergarten teacher, Anne says. Sylvia put on a Thanksgiving dinner for her students and their parents and Anne was there to help.

Herkey was a great guy, Steve says. "He was so good to his mother-in-law." Steve used to tell him "when you die you're going straight to heaven."

Sylvia taught Anne to sew and crochet. They went to cooking school together for a year. "She's a grand person," Anne says. "She'd do anything for anybody."

When Steve and Anne's grandson was tragically killed in an auto accident, Sylvia and Herkey were there. And when Sylvia and Herkey's granddaughter and her boyfriend went missing overnight in Allegany State Park, Steve and Anne were at their side until the pair was found safe the next morning. Through deaths of parents and grandparent they stood side by side.

Sylvia called Anne the sister she never had. Anne and Sylvia had birthdays a day apart; Herkey and Steve's were a few days apart.

Around 2000 the Smiths retired full time to Florida while the LaVoices rented an apartment there for a few winter months.

"You always said you were going to buy a house in Florida," Sylvia would tell them.

"Yes, when you find one across the street from you," Anne would reply.

One day Sylvia called—she'd found one. She got purchase papers ready, they went down for a weekend and signed the deal.

Once again neighbors, Steve and Herkey were regular cohorts as LaVoices continued as winter-only residents of

Florida. Herkey died suddenly overnight a few years ago. "Steve is lost down there now," Anne says.

Herkey's death also devastated Sylvia; they did everything together. Now Sylvia dwells in the fog of dementia, but "as bad as she is right now," Anne says, "she remembers me."

On friendship Steve says "It is everything."

He would also call Anne his best friend. As he went through a second round of knee surgery in a month "she's there for me. She always has been." He is close to tears. "You take a lot of things for granted. When I get on the pedal exerciser in middle of night she's right there.

"Friends are special in different ways.

"You don't think that you've had that interesting a life, then you start reminiscing. I can look around and say how lucky I am."

Chapter Eighteen

A friendship that can end never really began.
Publilius Syrus, 85-43 BC

Judy Shuler

Unexpected Endings

With the long view of time, it is sometimes surprising which friendships stumbled and fell and which endured.

Kaaren & Nancy & Me

Students come to college from diverse backgrounds with varying goals, so it's no surprise they scatter after graduation. Just trying to make it through required science classes consumed a lot of my attention, but I met two women with whom I felt a deep connection.

Kaaren and I met as freshmen at the University of Wisconsin, Madison. We moved into the then brand-new Chadbourne Hall, on the ninth floor. I was rooming with Carol, a high school friend, Kaaren lived down the hall. We shared the common bathroom, the cafeteria, the basic classes required of all freshmen. Both enrolled in home economics, we also attended the same introductory classes for our chosen major. We quickly bonded.

When Carol decided not to return to college the following fall, Kaaren and I became roommates at Chadbourne for the two coming years. We both focused on class work, granting little time to extra-curricular activities. One exception. Kaaren was an avid football fan and autumn Saturdays meant walking to home games at Camp Randall Stadium. She followed players and their lives like some people follow movie stars, and reeled off names I remember to this day. Her bass voice would be hoarse from yelling by the end of a game. It was impossible not to get caught up in her enthusiasm. Without her I surely would not understand the basics of football and still count it my favorite sport.

I had an early interest in architecture that was deepened by an icon in her home town of Spring Green, Frank Lloyd Wright's Taliesin East. Her mother worked for Wright as a young woman, Kaaren told me, and that personal connection cemented my life-long attraction to his work.

In our senior year a third student, Jan, joined us in renting an apartment off campus near the football stadium. Solid friends, we got on with none of the three-person drama that sometimes occurs. We were a formidable sight walking the sidewalk. At 5'9" I was the shortest and loved how people would turn and look at three tall women together.

Kaaren's brother, Don, was also a student at the university, a few years ahead of us. I had a huge crush on him, well before I was mature enough for a real relationship. When he earned his undergraduate degree he left school, but not my imagination. I knew the company he worked for and kept hoping I would see him again. Eventually Kaaren told me he was married and starting a family.

By my second year I gravitated to journalism with the dream of writing for magazines or newspapers. When I switched my major from home economics to journalism I met Nancy. I was country, she was city. We both joined a journalism sorority, Theta Sigma Phi, and were members of the planning committee for an awards banquet in our senior year. Maria von Trapp was guest speaker two years before the film *Sound of Music* was released. While I fretted about landing my first job after graduation, Nancy planned to join the newly formed Peace Corps. I liked working with her and getting to know her but thought it unlikely we would ever be in contact again.

Kaaren continued on in home economics. When I graduated I knew I was through with school, with no desire for a higher degree. Much as I cared about Kaaren and Jan, I also wanted to have a place of my own. I hoped Kaaren and I would stay in touch, but we set out on our own paths without looking back. I headed 260 miles from home for my first job in St. Paul, MN. Kaaren started teaching in Richland Center, about 25 miles from her home town.

Two years later I took off for Alaska and lost thought of contact. I was in a restaurant in Alaska's Matanuska Valley about a decade later and by coincidence struck up a conversation with a couple who lived in Spring Green. They knew Kaaren and said she was teaching. I was beside myself with excitement, wrote a note on a postcard with my address and asked them to deliver it to her. They promised they would. I didn't hear back.

As I began writing about friendship decades later, Kaaren and Nancy came to mind. I no longer needed a serendipitous meeting with neighbors, only the internet. I was ninety-five percent sure I'd found them both online. The unusual spelling of Kaaren's first name helped narrow her search and it didn't surprise me she was still in Spring Green. I remember her being quite homesick those first months in college and knew she was closely bound to her family.

Nancy was working in public relations in Chicago, which seemed consistent with where I'd expect her to be.

I sent each a handwritten note with a short summary of my life since college and telling them about my book. "I'm here to say hello because you were a special part of my life at UW," I wrote. I added I hoped they were doing well and I'd love to hear about their lives since we parted in school. My postal and email addresses were included.

Neither responded.

A few weeks after mailing the letters I had a vivid dream about Kaaren. She appeared to be about 40, wearing a large picture hat like she might don for a Kentucky Derby party. Her skin was flawless and smooth and she looked beautiful. She also seemed very happy, though we didn't talk about how she was or what she was doing.

Three years later I got an email with her name in the subject line. I was as excited as when I met her neighbors in Alaska. Perhaps she was at last answering or sending me a story about her own friendship.

When I opened the message it was a link to a funeral home and her obituary. It was signed only with the first name of her brother Don's wife.

She died in a nursing home, according to the story. I don't know how long she had been there, or the circumstances of her passing. I left a note on the website's tribute wall. And I sent an email back to her brother's wife expressing my deep appreciation for the contact. Did Kaaren ever see my letter? Was she already in failing health? I will never know but clearly Don saw it and felt I deserved notice of her passing. A thoughtful gesture from a long-ago crush that brought both sadness and gratitude.

***

Not all friendships end well. Sometimes they fade gradually. Sometimes they butt up against miscommunications and misunderstanding. Sometimes relationships fail to mature and shed high school persona. Sometimes they end with a thud. Names in this story have been changed.

Sarah & Mary Ellen

Mary Ellen was Sarah's best friend for their last two years of high school "despite the fact she was even more boy crazy than me–and I was pretty boy crazy," Sarah says.

"I guess most of us were at that age. But Mary Ellen could be really silly about it, at least that's what I thought. For example, why in the world would she want to be a cheerleader? Especially since this was the sixties, before cheerleaders had to be real athletes. I tamped down my disdain, probably because I hadn't quite reconciled how my own appearances in school plays were really any different. And, besides, hanging out with Mary Ellen was fun. We would borrow her dad's car and circle the A&W with the Beatles on the radio and us bouncing and laughing and hoping to see some boys. If we did, Mary Ellen would whip off her glasses and make me steer from the passenger seat as she flashed her biggest smile and I, terrified that I was gonna run over someone, kept my eyes on the road. For some reason, that didn't really bother me. I figured she'd outgrow all that once we started college and things got more serious. Boy, was I wrong about that."

In their freshman year Sarah began to focus on a career as an actor and, "to my horror, Mary Ellen chose to become a Pom-pom Girl. No athletic skill was required, the skirts were really short, and the smiles were really big. Mary Ellen could do that. I was embarrassed for my friend. Hadn't she even *heard* of the women's movement? This was also when she began dashing into the ladies' room between classes to check her hair and freshen her lipstick. What was happening? As I grew more and more serious about a life in art, she seemed to be living back in the fifties. Our paths had diverged irretrievably. I stopped calling her.

"About half-way through that first semester, Mary Ellen showed up at my house and wanted to talk. She looked really sad, and said she didn't understand why I had pulled away from her. I admit to feeling quite superior as I calmly explained that her values were just too different from my own now. I made no effort to comfort or reassure her. I was certain that the break was for the best and I wished her luck. She left the house in tears. I felt very righteous. Let her prance for the boys, I had more important goals for my future."

It was ten years before they spoke again.

The funeral for Sarah's father brought her back home. "Because I was feeling sentimental, I called Mary Ellen's parents who still lived in the area," she says. "I had always loved them, and had spent many happy hours in their home. They welcomed me back as though there had never been a split, and they told me about Mary Ellen's life married to a man working for a government agency in South America. They assured me that she would love to hear from me."

In her first letter Sarah apologized and took full responsibility for having ended their friendship years earlier. Mary Ellen's response was gracious and enthusiastic. They continued to correspond, and met for dinner a couple of times when Mary Ellen got back to the states.

"We were both having interesting lives, and our conversations were full of stories about our travels." Mary Ellen was heading for a country in Africa, her husband's new posting, and planned to climb Mt. Kilimanjaro while on the continent. Would Sarah like to do that with them? "I jumped at the idea. We continued to correspond and when the time finally came, I didn't hesitate."

By then Sarah was living in Panama, had just left her job as assistant to Dame Margot Fonteyn on her cattle farm, and was not making much salary.

"However, Mary Ellen's offer was generous—if I could get myself to Africa, they would take care of other expenses. Clearly, she was as eager to spend time with me as I was with her. After borrowing a bit from a friend, I had just enough for my $2,000 plane ticket."

Mary Ellen met Sarah at the airport, drove them to her home, and introduced Sarah to her husband, Bill, and their British friend Ian, a younger man who was joining them on this safari. This was a farewell to Africa adventure for Ian as his job was ending and he was heading back to England. Two days later they were off, the car packed with two tents, foodstuffs, cooking equipment, jerry cans of drinking water and all the necessaries for a two-week safari to Tanzania and the highest mountain on the continent.

The first night they made camp, Mary Ellen and Sarah gathered firewood while the men set up the tents, one for them, and the other for the women.

"After our dinner and washing up, I was surprised to see Mary Ellen and Ian strolling off in the dark together for a walk in the bush. Bill and I sat by the fire chatting until finally we said our 'good nights,' and each headed off to our respective tents. I was asleep and didn't hear Mary Ellen's return."

This set the nightly pattern for the trip.

"But just as surprising, Mary Ellen seemed to be constantly preening and flirting with Ian, clearly preferring his company to that of her husband's or mine. I could understand if this attention was due to her friend's soon departure from Africa, but to the exclusion of me and her husband? Bill certainly didn't seem to be bothered in the least by his wife's behavior. Was it my imagination? But why had she invited me to come to Africa if she was going to direct all her attention elsewhere?

"Was I included merely to keep Bill company? I was uncomfortable with the arrangement even if her husband was not. And what of Ian? What was his position? To be fair, he did not appear overly attentive to Mary Ellen. Except for their evening strolls, which she seemed to initiate, I never saw him actively courting her attention. Although he never sought my company nor made any effort to engage me in conversation, he interacted with Bill as a friend. Was Bill oblivious? Did he and Ian have some sort of understanding about Mary Ellen? The actual dynamic among those three was something I never discovered, but that Mary Ellen craved Ian's focus was clear. How far they took it was a mystery. I wasn't offended–I have a *laissez faire* attitude toward other people's relationships–but I was lonely.

"For me, the safari had been an opportunity to mend fences and have long, catch-up conversations with my friend, and she had given me every indication that she wanted that too. But now, when I attempted to engage Mary Ellen, she seemed uninterested, even distant. Instead, she seemed to be replicating her old need to be desirable to men–and I was relegated to the position of husband-minder. I was still steering the car while she smiled at the boys."

In preparation for their first country border crossing and a possible search by border guards, it was deemed necessary to hide any American dollars and British pounds as deeply inside their gear as possible before again strapping the load onto the roof of the car. If the money were buried deep enough, it might appear too much trouble for the guards to make them unpack everything for inspection. They would keep only a reasonable amount of Zambian money accessible. If their western money were found, they would be forced to exchange it for the local currency—one way the Third World is able to get its hands on stronger capital.

"As Mary Ellen's invited guest, I had brought very little money, only a bit of pocket change," Sarah says. "When the others realized this, a subtle, but palpable shift occurred. I began to feel more and more isolated from the group. I had no way to extricate myself as we were a long way from telephones and airports. Mary Ellen grew even more distant, I became increasingly depressed and finally I became really sick.

"We had reached the hotel at the base of Kilimanjaro, the starting point for our ascent. In the middle of that first night, I awoke in the room I shared with Mary Ellen feeling my whole body itching as though being attacked by a thousand mosquitoes. I leaped from my bed and switched on the light. The person I saw in the mirror was unrecognizable. My left eye was swollen closed and the right side of my upper lip was bulging from my mouth. I pulled off my pajamas to discover what looked like a giant red snake twisting around my torso. Mary Ellen, awake now, was staring in disbelief. Neither of us knew what to do. We could see no sign of insects on my body nor in the bed. Heading for the bathtub, I braved the brown water that came from the faucet and began vigorously wiping my body with a wash cloth. I had to relieve the terrible itching and remove any microscopic form of life that might be present and rendering me a monster. After more than an hour, I returned to my bed, discarded the hotel sheets in favor of my sleeping bag, but was unable to sleep."

When Bill and Ian came next morning, they were as astounded as Mary Ellen and Sarah had been to see what she looked like. The itching subsided a bit and she skipped breakfast in favor of more sleep. The swelling began to lessen throughout the day, and, although quite tired, she ventured out around the grounds by herself. The others had dispersed hours earlier to explore the hotel compound and surrounding country. They were to meet their porters and start their climb the next day.

"That night the horror repeated itself, with the swellings appearing on the opposite side of my face. My right eye was swollen shut and my lower lip distended hideously. The huge welts on my body returned along with the almost unbearable itching. I didn't know if Mary Ellen was awake as I attempted once more to wipe away the poison. It was hours before I was able to sleep, and then, fitfully."

Two elderly British women owned and ran the hotel where they stayed. Sarah sought their help the next morning, but they claimed to have no experience with this condition. Exhausted from lack of sleep and the persistent itching, she begged them to see if there was a doctor among their guests. There wasn't.

"I was terrified of being left behind at the hotel, missing my chance to climb the mountain. My three companions were somewhat concerned, but it seemed they were thinking of the cost of my climb being lost, rather than any true sympathy for my illness. It was clear that if I was to climb Kili, I was to do it without any real encouragement or moral support from them."

By the departure hour swellings and itching were again reduced, and although extremely tired and weak, she was excited and energized enough to start off with the group.

"While the other porters ran ahead to prepare each night's camp and meal for us, the head porter, Joachim, stayed with us, guiding us throughout the four days up and three days down. Over the course of those seven difficult days, Joachim became my true and only friend, somehow intuiting that I was a pariah and in need of companionship. I will never forget that beautiful human being."

The swellings and itching returned every night of the climb, but to a lesser degree each time. She was growing weaker from lack of sleep.

"We were aware that the fourth day of the climb is the most difficult, extremely steep and covered in scree; climbers slip back one step for every two forward. Due to oxygen deprivation, many have banging headaches throughout that final day of climbing. Many find themselves throwing up repeatedly. I did both. Were it not for Joachim, I would never have made the summit. Once I did, I collapsed and slept for several hours. Mary Ellen used my camera and snapped a photo of me sound asleep in the snow. I still have that picture.

"Joachim woke me to begin our descent in the dark, which had to be accomplished while there was still enough moonlight to see the path. The others had left much earlier, and Mary Ellen was in the bunk room when I stumbled in. My body shaking, I sat on a bed and sobbed. It was over. I was sick and alone, but I had done it. Even though I was well aware that without Joachim's support, I would have failed, still I had made it to the top. Mary Ellen sat next to me and kindly put her arms around me for which I was incredibly grateful. It meant everything just to feel a human touch after so many days with none. Her solicitude, however, did not extend past that night.

"The depression, illness and climb had weakened me so that my body seemed susceptible to any onslaught. On the return trip, we visited Ngorongoro Crater and while there I experienced a mysterious series of non-stop burping. I was unable to halt this weird attack and was further weakened by it to the extent that I was forced to remain at the hotel the next day, resting and drinking Pepto-Bismol while the others visited another game park. The next morning, we began our return road trip."

Mary Ellen and Sarah had originally planned one more trip for just the two of them to Victoria Falls, but Sarah begged off.

"I was eager to get away from Africa and Mary Ellen. Ian was flying back to England the next day and I hitched a ride to the airport for an earlier flight home. Because I had a stopover in London, he and I were on the same plane, but, pointedly, we chose not to sit together."

About a month later Sarah received a letter from Mary Ellen.

"She explained that while they had wanted to cover any expenses while I was staying at their home, once we were on the road they had fully expected me to pay my own way, especially for the climb and the game parks. She told me that without any funds, I had put the entire trip in jeopardy, and that she and Bill had been forced to borrow four hundred dollars from Ian to cover my cost. She found it hard to believe that I would have expected her to pay for my safari.

"Naturally I was horrified. I immediately wrote her back, explaining that I had indeed mistakenly understood that she was offering to pay for my safari. Knowing how much I was spending just to fly to Africa, I truly thought she wanted to pick up the rest so that she and I could share this special adventure. Why, I asked her, had she not told me of this right away so that I could have apologized, explained the miscommunication and assured her that I would repay her as soon as I returned to the states? Instead, I had been treated as an outcast without any explanation. I enclosed the four hundred for Ian, and asked her to tell me right away how much I owed her."

Mary Ellen didn't write back.

"I am glad I got to see some of Africa, but it really was not worth the toll on my physical and mental health for the period I was there. Besides abandoning me, Mary Ellen's behavior with Ian convinced me that she was still choosing to be that pom-pom girl, focusing her energy on attracting the boys. Once again I would cut ties with my old high school friend, but this time it was different. I did not feel at all superior or righteous. Just sad."

Sarah never heard from Mary Ellen again.

Chapter Nineteen

Things are never quite as scary when you've got a best friend.

Bill Watterson

Friends at My Fingertips

Far-away friends offer much-needed support through phone calls, emails, texts. But it is the friends close at hand that get you through the day and through the night.

HIS FRIENDS & MINE

Fred retired in May to spend the summer with his mother in New York. She was declining in health and alone after the death of his dad, and he wanted to spend some quality time with her. It also gave him an opportunity to re-connect with friends dating back to his high school days. I continued running my tour business in Alaska. We both spent that Christmas with her, then continued on to London for a theater tour with the local college. In February she passed.

We began summering in his family home, returning to Juneau in the fall where I continued to work and he sang with local choral groups. Summers were like an extended vacation, with pre-set beginning and ending dates. Bookends, I called them. While still at work in Alaska I researched summer theater and concert performances in New York and nearby Erie, PA, and Niagara on the Lake, Ontario, and ordered tickets online. Once in New York I checked the Dunkirk newspaper's calendar of events every day. We planned lunches and dinners with friends, making sure we spent time with all of them before leaving again in the fall.

Fred called our summer home "Sanctuary," and I made a wooden sign that still hangs over the front steps.

Gradually we put our imprint on the farmhouse and made it our own. Twelve years later I retired and we moved to New York full time. More remodeling converted it from what felt like a vacation home to a year-around residence. Gone were the heavy drapes and small windows, in came picture and bow windows that brought the outdoors inside.

Five years after our move Fred fell suddenly and gravely ill. We got daily phone calls, emails and texts from Alaska and around the country. But it was friends at my fingertips who came to our side and never left. Who overwhelmed me with their kindness and touched me to the core. Food, shopping, transportation, errands, and simply being there.

They started out as his friends—sometimes I still thought of them that way. But it was a specious distinction. Friendship cannot be assigned or possessed, has no boundaries.

Barb, who recently lost her own husband, went to Walmart for shoes to fit Fred's swollen feet for a trip to Roswell Park Cancer Institute in Buffalo when I no longer wanted to leave him alone. She picked up hand lotion for me because I was washing my hands more often, and the Root Rescue I requested. My hair was unkempt, I kept wearing the same jeans and mock tees. There was little time for personal care. I'm in awe of those who are care-givers for years and wonder how they keep a balance.

It was just before Christmas. Sisters Elsie and Lynn, both widows, stopped by after church. They would drive us to Roswell for a test on Monday and bring us back on Tuesday. Lynn brought Fred's Christmas present, a hand-knit white scarf to go with the black leather jacket he'd ordered when he still felt better. She had taken me to the drug store for prescription injections and to the grocery store for apple juice and watermelon. Elsie sat with Fred while I went to the bank for cash. Dean brought Marie's homemade beef soup and also offered to drive us to Buffalo as needed.

Comfort food is more than idle cliché. Friends made it their mission to keep us fed.

Sally brought by a big container of chicken soup, the first food he showed any interest in except watermelon for days. The day before Christmas she brought homemade tomato soup, one of his favorites, because she didn't want us to be without something to eat on Christmas Eve. A new recipe, she said, starting with roasting tomatoes and including fresh basil.

After the 7 p.m. Christmas Eve service, Elsie and her daughter Jill brought dinner: thick stuffed pork chops, potatoes au gratin, Brussels sprouts, whipped orange Jell-O with miniature marshmallows, spritz cookies. In better times, Fred would have counted the pork chops and potatoes a special treat.

On Christmas day Sandy brought her grandmother's white chocolate pie. In the evening, Sally brought plates of Christmas dinner from her family gathering—prime rib, twice-baked potatoes, carrots, and a tossed salad. Long-time friends now living in the Midwest and West, Grant, and his children Ellice and Joel called for Christmas. Fred had been reluctant to tell some people he was sick, so we finally gave them the news.

Christmas passed. The following day Elsie came by, picked up a grocery store list and box for mailing at the post office, then returned with the groceries and cleaning supplies. Groceries were minimal. Fred was eating almost nothing and I was eating bits of what people brought by plus all the accumulated Christmas cookies and sweets.

Fred still liked milk shakes, and Elsie promised and delivered a chocolate milk shake from McDonald's. Barb called, as she had almost daily, and brought potato leek soup. Everyone was bringing soup, which turns out to be a good choice for someone with little appetite, something I need to remember in the future.

Sally called to see if we had a taste for anything. I told her I'd love a green salad—she said she'd already thought to do it. She came by with an apple/chicken salad from Wendy's. I had half for lunch, and have likely never appreciated a salad as much as this one. Down to 138 pounds that morning, my lowest in over three decades.

Midway between Christmas and New Year's Day high winds caused a power outage beginning at 5 a.m. Three poles were split in front of a nearby greenhouse. By then Fred was on full-time oxygen, using an electric concentrator. I kept calling the power company and estimates for restoration of power were pushed back each time. I'd called George and Judy to see if they had power, they later came by and offered to take us to their house for duration of the outage. By early afternoon I was chilled, worried about getting sick myself and nervous about keeping oxygen tanks going. I called the medical supply company for more and they brought four large E tanks. Even on full power, not puff mode, they drained down at alarming rate. Fred didn't want to leave the house, but he knew I did. I called George and Judy back. We loaded up concentrator, extra tank, change of clothes and medication, but left crucial things behind, like a raised toilet seat. She served soup and apple pie; he ate only a little soup. Their recliner worked okay, but was unfamiliar. Getting in and out of their car, a low Mercury sedan, was painful. Back home after power was restored Fred said "never again."

Another day Sally ran in with ham dinner—ham, mashed potatoes, corn. She kept me in food; I knew I'd really miss her when she returned to Florida for the winter.

On New Year's Eve day Sally called about bringing dinner; I suggested another salad. Elsie and Lynn came in the afternoon, before their annual New Year's Eve movie and dinner with their sister Carol. Elsie brought the lemons and urinal I requested. Barb and her son Doug brought a recliner for Fred to try. Jan called and she and Bill brought chicken noodle soup.

Two days into the New Year Sally dropped off salad and soup from Applebee's. Lynn and Elsie brought milk shakes from McDonald's and stayed while I cleaned the sidewalk of snow, did laundry in the basement, got mail from across Route 20. Fred hardly spoke to anyone, mostly kept his head down, chin on chest, sleeping. But the milkshake, vanilla and chocolate blended, piqued his interest. Elsie also brought a tied fleece blanket she won at a shower, saying it was bigger than the one he was using. When I finished my tasks he said "I have to rest now," as though telling them to leave. They did.

That evening while trying to move from walker to toilet, he slid to floor. I didn't know how to get him up, and called Bobby and Sandy. Thankfully they were home and helped lift him back to sofa arm where he could try again. I had worried that he was so weak he could barely stand and anticipated this happening. I wished his local oncologist would send him to nearby Brooks Memorial Hospital for feedings to build up his strength. Later he slipped to floor again. Bobby was sleeping so I called Rod. Together we could not lift him. Next call 911, back to Brooks ER. He was admitted to a room at 4 a.m., a private room with recliner for me.

The next day Elsie and Lynn came to the hospital after church, bringing a sandwich for me and freeing me to go home for shower, laundry and errands.

Monday they returned after an eye appointment in Erie, bringing a sandwich, our mail, bottled lemonade from a store and Pepsi and terry cloth bibs from our house. At the house they also wheeled the garbage can to the road for pick up.

Tuesday Lynn brought me a chicken croissant sandwich, and stayed with Fred while I went home to shower and pick up extra underwear. I sensed this may be my last time to leave him that long.

On Wednesday, Bill stopped by after therapy downstairs at the hospital. Al walked up for a short visit with what must have been great difficulty due to his own limited mobility. Both were Fred's high school classmates. Jan stopped in the afternoon to ask if I needed anything. I'd forgotten it was bridge day for Elsie and Lynn, who usually brought a sandwich for my lunch. She'd already left when I looked the clock, 1:45 p.m., and called her cell to ask for a sandwich and black coffee from Tim Hortons. Never missing a day, Lynn and Elsie came in late afternoon after bridge.

Thursday, Elsie came about noon with a Waldorf salad she made and Tim Hortons mac & cheese courtesy of Natalie, one of our bridge partners, because she "can't do anything else." Natalie was home-bound caring for her own husband. Calls continued from other states.

Another day. Jan brought Tim Hortons coffee and a glazed donut, Bill stopped after heart health exercise on first floor. Lynn came for respite and brought a sandwich courtesy of Natalie, while I left to search for waterproof bibs in stores, then went to Tim Hortons for chili for supper because I don't mind it cold. I drove to the Dunkirk pier on Lake Erie, one of my favorite spots, for a short walk outside. There was a cool breeze, almost no birds in sight. I called Kathy in Juneau and broke down for the first time. George and Judy stopped by in mid-afternoon, offering to bring food or anything else I needed.

Saturday, the weekend, though like any other day. Bill and Jan stopped with coffee, muffin and a lavender and white bouquet in a straw basket from Fresh & Fancy Flowers. A small lavender butterfly was tucked inside. I had been thinking about a pupa breaking through into a butterfly like the process of dying and trying to emerge to the other side. But I didn't tell them that because I thought I might break down. They have been so faithful in stopping by—it touches and humbles me. Elsie stayed while I went home to shower. My 100-year-old neighbor Liz called to ask how Freddie was doing; I told her bluntly he was dying.

When Lynn came on Sunday, I went to Demetri's On the Lake for a rare lunch away from the hospital. Driving past Wright Park on the way back, I watched snow and wind coming in as water washed over the breakwall. Emails, calls and texts continued: Karen, Grant, Jan, Donna, Kathy,

Cheryl, Hildegard, Helena, Geri. Pastor Barb stopped by the hospital, saying she would be glad to do a memorial service for Fred. As a teenager he was an active member of her Tri-Church congregation but we had not joined any church since moving back here. Still it was important for me to have his service in a church, not just a funeral home. Donna, a long-time friend from Juneau, invited me to come up for a few weeks this summer. Travel to see friends was the one thing that seemed to matter as I looked ahead. I finally called my cousin Kris, and Joanne, his former classmate and friend in business college; I thought they were the last I needed to call.

Monday, schools and events were closed due to wind and snow. A blizzard moved in last night and I needed to go to the parking lot to brush snow from the car while it was still loose. I didn't have my fleece pants or warm gloves or headwear—it was 50 degrees yesterday—and didn't look forward to venturing outside but finally forced myself. Would I remember where I parked? I'd moved it so many times in the hospital parking lot in the last week. And it was white. Could I see it under all the snow? Thankfully Fred had distinctive red and blue military veteran plates so I found it easily. Finding the snowbrush was another matter. Not in the trunk, but fortunately in the back seat. I brushed it off, cleaned the windshield wipers. Back inside I went down to the basement dining room for a breakfast tray to take back to the room. Pancake special—not my first choice, but I took it with bacon and coffee. I headed to the elevator when someone grabbed the edge of my tray. It was a nurse who had been looking for me. She came to tell me he passed while I was out of the room.

I texted Elsie, adding "don't even think of leaving home." Dunkirk and Fredonia were nearly shut down by poor driving conditions. When I didn't hear back I felt bad that I had texted, not called, with such defining news. I called her house, then Lynn's. No answer. Shortly they walked in the door.

By then I'd spilled my entire cup of coffee over the floor, and nibbled on bacon. They urged me to finish breakfast. I wondered if I should feel guilty about eating just after he passed. A few years earlier he had donated his body to the University at Buffalo Anatomical Gift Program for teaching or research upon his death. I was proud of his decision and wanted to make sure the hospital followed up before I left. But an aide said we had to leave first to make room for a separate bed to transport him.

Lynn rode home with me so I wouldn't be alone, Elsie arrived at the house first. The storm had let up from early morning so visibility and roads were much improved. They came inside, asked what they could do. The house was a mess, stuff thrown everywhere. I decided I'd like Christmas cards and trees taken down. Decorations were all in place before he fell so ill. The bright light given off by two small trees was a saving grace when he did not want to be in darkness through the night. They helped remove and box ornaments and the trees.

The next day Marie and Dean sent flowers, a white bouquet from the floral shop. Charlotte remembered that Fred, a good customer, usually ordered white flowers from her. Blizzard conditions returned, driving was terrible. Rod drove in with warm scalloped potatoes and croissants, in thick of the storm. Elsie emailed, Lynn texted, willing to do anything, even on a day like this. Joanne called from Virginia. I said I knew she and her son came to see Fred on visits the past few years but hoped they would come to see me too. She said they would. She pondered how something prompted her to write Fred a few years earlier after span of many years. She said she was glad to have the last years with him, and that I had come into their lives.

A week after his passing was our 47th wedding anniversary. My cousins in Chicago sent a green plant assortment in a basket. When one, a peace lily, later bloomed to my surprise, I sent Kris a photo by text. Fred is sending his love, she replied. Sandy, the craftiest friend I have, brought a quilted wall hanging of animals in winter, tavern ham, and a slice of pumpkin pie.

In the aftermath Jenean dropped off a sympathy card, journal and pen from my Write Now writers' group in Brocton, acknowledging that sometimes even writers are at a loss for words. Des sent a dozen roses in multi colors with an endearing note. Cheryl emailed, asking when his service would be so she and Jon could have moment of silence and prayer at their home in Arizona. It was scheduled a few weeks after his passing, when out-of-town friends could come.

The night before his service, I served a spaghetti dinner for my family and our friends both local and from afar. It was the meal he was best known for, served countless times for co-workers, houseguests, pinochle partners and birthday celebrations. The last meal of Fred's spaghetti sauce and meat balls, made and frozen the previous June. I filled two crock pots with sauce and 60 meat balls.

Though no longer an intact family, Grant and Karen came with their grown children, Joel, Derek and Ellice; Derek's newly pregnant wife, Ashley; and Grant's fiancé Kirsten. They flew in from four different states. When the children were young the family came on vacation every summer. Fred planned a full round of activities for them: amusement parks when they were little, tickets to plays as they grew older. He even arranged a trip for all of us to New York City one year. Now that they were grown and had lives of their own, Fred said he never expected to see them again. I hoped he could see how they all came for him now. If Fred's final gift was bringing them together he would be very pleased.

Pete and Doris drove from New London, CT. Doris and Fred grew up together; Fred met Pete in the army and introduced them. My cousin Emory, his wife Trudie and my sister-in-law Helena arrived by road from Wisconsin after an overnight at South Bend, IN.

Barb brought big containers of orange-cranberry scones and date muffins for breakfast the next two days. Lynn brought a huge salad. For dessert, we had chocolate cheesecake from Des, and Sandy's white chocolate almond pie, both from Christmas.

The day of the service, I loaded photos in a plastic laundry basket, along with his American Legion hat, white satin stole from Chautauqua Literary and Scientific Circle book club and a Messiah score, celebrating his love of reading and music, and comradery of the Legion. I wore the white tunic Helena crocheted for me years earlier. White was our color. White cars, white house, white walls and furnishings, the white flowers he often brought me.

I wanted music to be a main part of his service as it was in his life. Lucy looked directly at me when she sang *Amazing Grace*. I'd told her beforehand it was Fred's favorite hymn and she said she was honored to sing it in his remembrance. A young woman I'd recently met sang *On Eagle's Wings*, a song Fred and I had sung in a church choir in Juneau.

I was composed through the service, thinking surely people were watching me, until Derek's touching eulogy calling Fred the grandfather he'd never known. I and much of the congregation teared up.

Marie Z. and Marie S. brought food to the luncheon at the Legion following his service. Friends most visibly shaken by his death were people who'd known him a very long time, but were living elsewhere—Pete and Doris, Des, Donna, Grant.

We'd been lucky with weather in always problematic January. Sunday's weather report included snowstorms in Wisconsin on Tuesday. My family planned to stay another day, but I urged an earlier departure for their two-day trip and they left that afternoon. Elsie and Lynn stopped by to say good-bye to everyone. By 2 o'clock, everyone was gone. It was such a mild day—55 degrees—that I put on a jacket and went outside for a walk along the creek behind our house.

When I went to the mail box some days and a snowstorm later I saw, half covered with snow, the thank-you note I'd written to Derek and Ashley that the mailman must have dropped when retrieving it from the box. How easily I could have missed it. Fred? I want to feel his presence. Am I looking right past it? Is he thinking "What do I have to do to get her attention?"

In early February, a small heart-shaped box filled with chocolates arrived from Karen, ensuring that this year I would again receive a valentine. And a valentine came from Trudie and Emory, saying that first holidays are hard.

Donna called; she was still in Seattle after back surgery a week earlier. She worked with Fred and was much affected by his passing, and has been keeping in touch. Kathy called every week. She asked if a trip to Juneau was in my plans and I assured her it was. I told her I was making progress; I could talk to her without breaking down, but I'm still tired, and not able to focus. She assures me of course that is true, will be so for a while, and it's okay.

From the memorial card I made up for his service:

<u>Friendship is a Sheltering Tree</u>
"From home-made soups, scalloped potatoes and deviled eggs to sandwiches, coffee and donuts, non-stop phone calls, emails and texts, running errands, shopping, transportation to appointments, flowers, just being at our side, it was support of friends and family who made this journey bearable. Deepest thanks to you all."

And from my first Christmas card alone:

From We to Me

"This has been a year of adjustment as I walk a new path with Fred's passing in January. It has been possible because you remind me over and over that I do not walk it alone. To say thank you does not begin to express all you mean to me."

Chapter Twenty

Dogs have a way of finding the people who need them, filling an emptiness we don't even know we have.

Thom Jones

Pets As Friends

Do dogs merit a place in a book about friendship? For many of us, the answer is an unqualified yes! Will Rogers (and my neighbor Rod, a pillar in his Episcopal Church) said "if there are no dogs in Heaven, then when I die I want to go where they went."

TUCKER COMES HOME

Tucker came into our lives in a time of sadness.

When my mother-in-law's health declined, my husband retired and went home to spend the summer with her. The following February she passed. In May we traveled across country in our mini-van to the now-empty house where his parents had lived. The stress of loss and change hovered and bore down as we settled in for the summer.

One August morning I picked up the Dunkirk *Observer* and was startled to see a photo with the headline "For Adoption." The subject was nearly the mirror image of Gus, the Dachshund-Chihuahua we'd lost a decade earlier.

I was the first to call the shelter and the next day we drove to the Northern Chautauqua Canine Rescue Center near Westfield to meet him.

A volunteer brought from the back a small armful of smooth black fur with a nylon bone held tightly in his teeth, and placed him in my arms. Instinctively I knew he was what we needed at that point in our lives. Perhaps he needed us too.

A few weeks later we drove and ferried 3,500 miles back across country to our Juneau home. We were unsure how the year-old Tucker would travel, but he took to it immediately. I checked AAA guidebooks for dog-friendly motels, not as common as they are today. Once checked in, we kept close watch to quell barking as other guests moved past our room. He took note, but barked only briefly.

We boarded the Alaska Marine Highway in Prince Rupert, B.C., for the final segment of our trip. When the ferry made port calls we'd retrieve him from our van and take him outside to relieve himself. He was compliant but subdued. Already he seemed to understand what it meant to be en route between two fixed points.

Tucker adapted quickly to his new Alaskan home. Soon he was chasing red squirrels and digging roots at the base of spruce and hemlock that filled our back yard. He sailed off the deck catching Pine Siskin in mid-flight, a shock and embarrassment to me as an active member of the local Audubon chapter.

Rescue animals come with histories and baggage we rarely know. Tucker seemed inordinately timid at times. He was dead last when I enrolled him in an obedience class and his hunting instinct always won out over responding to our call.

We spent every summer in New York thereafter. For the next 11 years he was the consummate traveler, flying at our feet beneath the seat between Juneau and Buffalo or Erie each spring and fall. He entered his Sherpa® bag without coaxing, and when the 14-16 hour trip commenced he curled up and silently waited for release at his destination. Fred often flew to New York a month before I did. When I'd walk through the airport terminal carrying Tucker in his black bag, Fred would whistle and Tucker rocked the whole bag in excited anticipation.

In his natal home he pounced on chipmunks and field mice, cowered in thunder storms and rolled over and over on grass. He moved between the disparate climate and landscapes of our two homes seamlessly, and made us smile every day.

A house sitter stayed in our Juneau house while we were away. One year she hung a bird feeder in the back yard, just off the deck. On my first day back I slid open the sliding glass doors in the still-dark September morning, grateful for the fenced yard. In New York he always had to be walked on a leash, here he could run free. Tucker charged off the deck, full hunter mode, as a black bear stood under the feeder just yards away. It may have been my screaming at Tucker that made the bear run away. Surely as Tucker dreamed that night, it was his prowess that quickly dispatched the bear through the wooded yard and over the five-foot chain link fence.

When Fred took Tucker for walks on a path along the Mendenhall River, he raced through flocks of ravens nearly as big as he, his all black coat disappearing from sight among them.

The Chilkat River near Haines attracts a gathering of some 3,000 bald eagles in October and November. I'd led photo tours there several years, but one year decided to go up with three other women just for fun. It was four and one-half hours from Juneau by ferry. We sailed to Haines Sunday morning and weren't due back until after midnight on Monday.

During their daily walk that Monday, Fred took Tucker for a walk near the fish hatchery, a departure from their usual path. It was a frosty morning and Fred slipped on black ice. After the fall, his left ankle pointed south and the sole of his foot pointed west. All three ankle bones were broken, though they didn't pierce skin. Because it was the Veteran's Day holiday, there weren't many other people around. He crawled to the car on his backside by himself, climbed inside, and drove himself to the hospital. Fortunately, it was just across the main highway and up the hill. It was focusing on Tucker, on keeping him close by and safe, that likely saved him from going into shock, Fred would later say. When he drove to the emergency entrance and honked the horn, staff first waved at him, then told him he was in a no-parking area. When he said he had broken his ankle, they told him he would have to park the car, and they would come pick him up.

Then there was the problem of Tucker still inside the car and me 90 miles away. Former fellow employees came to the rescue, driving the car home and getting Tucker inside the house, though they could barely stand to look at Fred's twisted foot before surgery straightened it out. Tucker could be standoffish and was indifferent to those who befriended him, but we were grateful.

I got the message of some of what transpired as we checked in for the return ferry in Haines Monday evening. Cell phones were not yet common, but thanks to someone who had one, I was able to talk to Fred in the hospital from the ferry parking lot. The ferry was an hour late in departing, then one hour out of Haines we returned to evacuate a crew member who became ill and was subsequently flown to Juneau by Coast Guard helicopter. The ferry eventually docked in Juneau at 4 a.m. Tuesday and at 8 a.m. I headed for the hospital.

Fred spent just one night in the hospital and returned home Tuesday afternoon. Three hours in surgery, a metal plate and six screws later, Tucker delightedly snuggled close and kept Fred constant company on the downstairs sofa.

Maneuvering was more difficult than he anticipated. The surgeon, in town from Seattle to fill in for the vacationing local bone specialist, said it would be a month before he could put the lightest pressure on the injured leg, and a year before it was back to normal. Fred would feel those screws, especially in winter cold, ever after.

Tucker came to us in a time of transition. Eleven years later we faced another transition, leaving our home state of 45 years to make our New York summer home a year-around residence.

Perhaps Tucker sensed the upheaval ahead and felt he'd come full circle. Early on a Monday morning in mid-January, he grew gravely ill without advance warning and spiraled downward with no way back up. An ultra-sound showed an enormous growth in his spleen. That night we said a wrenching goodbye.

In the next two months we sorted and cleared our house of decades of memorabilia. We'd been putting off the daunting task, but somehow our loss and sadness spurred Fred into action. We fretted about the likelihood of selling in a crowded housing market. Within two weeks of our first showing we had an offer, substantially lower than our buyer-friendly asking price. At the urging of our realtor we reluctantly made a counter offer, still well below what we wanted. "I hope the deal falls through," I said. After round two of offer and counter-offer, I was relieved when it did.

Two weeks later we had a full price offer from Ben, a young man who worked in the veterinary clinic that cared for Tucker through the years.

I hoped another dog would find us, as Tucker did. Not a clone, but one whose personality could fill our home as his did. If so, I would believe Tucker had a role, just as I like to think it's no coincidence that Ben and Claire now live in our Juneau house.

In late afternoon walks in New York, Tucker would often lead me to our third and most distant meadow, separated from the second meadow by a grove of trees. "Walking to Florida," I called it. We scattered his ashes among the trees and nailed a homemade sign, Tucker's Grove, to an apple tree frequented by deer. Tucker was home.

***

About Tyler

From first we met, Tyler lived life at warp speed.

He was the second to come into our home from Northern Chautauqua Canine Rescue in Westfield. We'd lost our beloved Tucker, also from the shelter, a year and a half earlier and it was time to re-fill the void as only an animal can.

Tyler's winsome picture appeared in the newspaper ad for adoptable animals with the caption *What's not to like?*

What not indeed? He had a face that melted everyone who saw him. When Fred sat in a room with him to get acquainted and try each other out, Tyler raced around the room, then put his paw in Fred's hand in trust. It was a relationship meant to be.

Tyler came to us flawed. There were two scars on his back that looked to me like acid burns, though others thought rope burns or even bite marks. And there was kind of an indentation in his backbone. What happened to him in his first few months we could not know, but they did not seem to pain him and surely didn't slow him down.

Our first three dogs were dachshund blends, and with Tyler's big ears and long body, we thought that's what we were getting again. At least we hoped so. We loved their inquisitive personalities and bright minds. It soon became clear Tyler was nothing like his predecessors. He raced through the house like Billy in *The Family Circus*. Up, down, over, and around every possible obstacle. Chairs, sofa backs, beds, our carefully constructed barriers—he conquered them all with ease. Full speed, then collapse into a tired puddle.

Curious about who he really was, we opted for a DNA test. He proved half beagle, half miniature pinscher, a *meagle*. An internet search found others with his same beautiful markings, his same engaging expression.

Like all puppies, he decided everything was best tasted and chewed. Pencils, socks, towels, toilet paper. My flip phone was chewed beyond salvation, as was Fred's $1,800 hearing aide. But who could hold a grudge against someone as spirited as he? The incidents became part of his lore.

I'd never fully trained our previous dogs as much as I'd liked and determined this time would be different. When local obedience classes were announced, I was first to sign up. When he joined a half-dozen other puppies he was a stand-out, but not for the right reasons. He barked and pulled constantly and singled out another dog with whom to exchange not-so-friendly words. We had initially requested private lessons for him; after a few group classes the instructor heartily concurred. Yet as he grew older, he liked meeting other dogs and playing with them. It must have been a conflict between just those two.

Sit was easy, *stay* pretty much worked only when there were no distractions like other people in the house. Loose leash walking remained a foreign concept. There were just too many enticing smells for a breed that embodies two hunters. As he put nose to the ground through our fields, I wondered who had passed there that Tyler was sensing. Much as I tried to hold him back with me, other things were far more interesting. It was a never-ending tussle, though I gradually got him to slow down about half-way through our loop around four acres.

My internet searches for training tips to make him more compliant to our will yielded little result when I tried to apply them.

When workmen or male guests entered the house for the first time he quickly backed away, leading me to think his abuser had been male. But shortly he was willing to crawl into their laps or lean against them as hard as he could.

Steps lead into our full basement through a kitchen door, initially intimidating enough to leave him at the top looking down. One day two workmen and Fred went down for repairs, and Tyler put on his big boy pants and followed them down. Ever after, he went down daily with Fred to do the laundry.

Tyler and Fred were the closest of friends. He was soon trained to go directly from house to car for whatever errands that day required. Fred had an ever ready supply of cookies for whenever he had to leave Tyler in the car, nearly always leaving the car running with heater or air conditioner as the weather dictated. They took afternoon naps together. Fred routinely fed him dog food, and to my disapproval, snacks. Popcorn, potato chips, ice cream—some for him, some for Tyler. Tyler also got to do what Lynn called "pre-wash," clearing plates of food residue before they went into the dishwasher. He seemed perpetually hungry, eating whatever was in front of him and always wanting more. Was it another hang-over from his first few months of life?

Tyler loved people and commanded their attention. Tuesday pinochle nights regularly brought four other people into his fold. Two were his favorites. He and Elsie shared a special bond and she cared for him in her home when we were away. He'd leap, all 39 pounds of him, into her lap without warning. Anne satisfied one of his peculiarities. He was an unabashed breast man, laying his long snout against the biggest bosom he could find, while looking up innocently. Pinochle night also brought two bones to occupy him while we played, a pattern he soon figured out and demanded.

With me the relationship was more complicated. He was more stand-offish, though he would come close when he initiated it. During evening TV time he'd lay across my lap on the sofa, pushing against me as tight as he could. Or he'd crawl under the zebra afghan Helena made for him and press the full length of his body against my leg. But whenever I touched his back he would turn around and look at me with some apprehension. And if I approached him from the front he would get downright snappish. I held my breath when other people reached out to pet him, but his reaction was limited to me.

Thinking then that he must have been abused by a woman, I turned to a dog behavior trainer for advice. She advised that I condition him to associate touch with food from me. She assigned the Hand Monster exercise, named by her young daughter. Give him a piece of food, then touch him. The better the treat, the longer the touch. It will help remind him that being touched isn't bad and if he tolerates it he'll be paid, she explained. Tyler was having none of it. In the morning I'd feed him a small handful of dog food, a few pieces at a time. He'd have to nudge or lick my hand before each feeding. Still, it was always on his terms.

When I discussed it with our veterinarian, he saw it as a struggle for dominance between the two of us. I needed to remind Tyler that he was the dog, living on the floor, coming on the sofa only when invited, and generally being subservient. I began making him sit while I passed through the door first, even when letting him into the yard to relieve himself. He obediently complied, though in his mind he must have still been top dog because I could not bring my hand over his head to pet him without eliciting a sharp rebuke.

We accommodated each other's peculiarities. He let me attach collar and leash with no resistance, eagerly looking forward to every outing whether a walk or ride in the car. He would jump into my lap, but not linger; he'd lick my feet and ankles on the sofa and snuggle next to me on the sunroom settee while I worked on my laptop. If I reached toward him, he'd quickly jump off.

He took his job as watch dog seriously, barking at passing walkers and cyclers. I always felt more secure knowing he was on duty. Sometimes squirrels and chipmunks attracted his attention, sometimes he merely looked at them. When critters got under the sunroom floor, he tore carpet and scratched walls in a vain attempt to reach them.

One weekend we noticed Tyler, a perpetual jumping machine, was unable to use his back legs to jump up on the sofa. We thought he must have sprained a muscle in one of his many jumps, and took him to the veterinary clinic Monday morning. He got a pain killer and muscle relaxant along with orders for rest. We blocked off steps to the second story and kept him from the basement stairs. At first he jumped on sofa and chairs a few times and we thought he was recovering. But after Tuesday night pinochle, he declined rapidly. Wednesday night he couldn't lay down, and hobbled around the front room like a seal for most of the night. It was hard for him to walk at all, and getting up the stairs to the deck was barely doable. We took him to Orchard Park Veterinary Hospital, the Cleveland Clinic of the animal world, on Thursday morning.

They diagnosed it as a spinal cord problem. The only real solution the doctor could put forth was surgery. Any other measures would only retain or temporarily improve the status quo, which was unacceptable. Surgery would require crate rest for several weeks, carrying him up and down five steps to go in the yard for at least that long, and with no guarantee he would walk again. Cost in the end would approach $10,000. Given Tyler's normally hyperactivity and the expense, we made the wrenching decision to let him go. We hoped it was the right one for him as well as us. Then we questioned ourselves. Was it really?

Fred had a foreboding of what was to come. And from the beginning we wondered how scars and an indentation in his back might affect him some day. We just didn't expect it to come so quickly or at a young age. He was only 4 ½ years old.

That night the bed that usually held three of us held only two. I felt a cool breeze and looked up to see if the fan was running. It wasn't. It was the same cool breeze I felt when first entering their houses after my mother and mother-in-law passed.

I hope he forgives us. Though he often tried our patience, we gave him the best life we could.

Fred said a prayer to God to accept Tyler. May he run free, at warp speed, with no leash holding him back.

Epilogue

Tyler was far from mellow, a challenging member of the household. Two months later Fred was diagnosed with cancer and in increasing pain. Having Tyler in the household at that time would have been impossible. And given his antipathy toward me, it's doubtful I could have handled him on my own. As it became clear Fred's illness would overtake him, I said that I hoped the first faces Fred would see on the other side would be those of Tyler and Tucker, his constant, beloved companions in retirement.

I believe it was so.

***

And Now, Bentley

Empty bed. Empty house. Empty dog yard with no reason to close the gates. The void was palpable.

Four months later, on a Friday in May, Bentley's photo appeared in the newspaper ad for Northern Chautauqua Canine Rescue.

Lynn emailed and Elsie texted. "He looks perfect for you."

I filled out the online application that morning. In the evening I was surprised to get a phone call from Marcia at the shelter. Would I like to meet Bentley?

"I thought I'd come by during the afternoon open house," I said.

She suggested coming by 11:30 a.m., in case others were interested. I paced around the house, doing aimless errands, arriving shortly after 11.

As I walked in two volunteers were working on him in the reception area, cutting stitches that I imagined were from neutering, and inserting a microchip at which he protested loudly. I recognized him immediately from the newspaper photo.

When I saw him I couldn't speak and tried to hold back tears. Looking at him was like looking at Tyler, and Fred who loved him dearly. I couldn't help thinking they had engineered our meeting. Tyler had very similar markings though as an adult was twice the size of the already full-grown Bentley.

Marcia asked if I'd like to take him for a walk and attached a leash. I walked outside and broke down thinking of them both. Bentley was clearly filled with energy, tugging at the leash with strength that belied his 18-pound weight. He pulled toward the shelter, as volunteers all greeted him by name. I sat on a bench outside and he jumped into my lap.

I fretted about the timing. Originally I wanted to adopt a dog in the fall. There were so many things to do in summer and I already had travel plans in September. I was just beginning to find a deeper connection with the natural world around me, in part by being alone without distractions. Would I lose that? I requested a few days to think about it and asked if there was a lot of interest in him. Marcia said she'd gotten another application that morning.

On the way home I stopped at the Brocton library where I knew Elsie and Lynn were taking a class. I also knew they would try to talk me into taking Bentley.

I drove to the grocery store in Dunkirk, stopping first at a pet store for dog food and treats and a hedgehog squeak toy. I'd gotten rid of all our dog paraphernalia when we lost Tyler. Back home I cleared plants and table from the sunroom window, replacing them with a big ottoman topped by a throw, a place for Bentley to watch his world go by. Yet I was uneasy, even frightened by taking on this commitment by myself.

Sunday afternoon, armed with the hedgehog, I claimed him and brought him home. The shelter lent me a plastic crate for safe travel. When he failed to lift his leg on long walks outside but peed on a quilt in the kitchen and on a stair post, I went out to buy another wire cage, which we'd also given away, to start crate training anew. I wasn't certain if it was the stress of the past few days, or if he was never completely house trained or just forgot. One night a week or two later I left the cage door ajar, he quickly noticed, and claimed his new bed with me.

He also pulled mightily on the leash and I wanted to start loose leash training right away. He was inconsistent with sit and come commands. There was lots of work to do in this new phase of our lives.

Three years later he still pulls, following every scent like the hunting dog he is. Loose-leash walking is never going to happen. I haven't tested DNA like we did for Tyler, but based on previous dogs I believe he is a blend of Dachshund and Chihuahua with the former dominating. He does well with *sit* and *stay*, but *come* must be coupled with a treat.

He climbs into my lap whenever I sit down. He charms everyone he meets and climbs into any lap he sees. He makes me smile and laugh. The dog yard gates are again securely closed.

***

Everyone who has a pet has a story. The following stories include the heights and depths of what they bring to our lives.

Donner–An Unlikely Companion

By Jenean Roth

It took about eleven years after losing my Great Dane, 'Tino, to be ready for another companion. I would have loved another Great Dane but he was irreplaceable, so I thought I'd look for any large breed dog. I shopped pit bulls, German Shepherds, Dane mixes, anything large. It was just my two daughters and me and our house is very small, but I was looking big. We did have a big yard. The landlord didn't allow cats but did allow me one dog so I had to make it worth it.

I wanted the girls to want the dog as much as I did so we "shopped" together. The first stop was Tractor Supply Co. where the canine rescue was having a satellite adoption day. As I'm looking at the big dogs in the big cages, the girls were looking more at their eye level and height; small cages and small dogs. On the end of a big cage was a little cage with a blanket on it and a little dog cowering inside, silent and motionless. I thought the poor thing was embarrassed at the sweater they had put him in, the girls thought he was scared to death and lonely. They wanted him instantly. Me? Not so much. That dog didn't appeal to me at all. I really tried to distract the girls from him but they weren't going for it. They ended up begging for that dog for weeks.

"Mmmmaaammmaaaaa! You have to call them. Please check on him. Please."

I tried every procrastination trick I could while at the same time figuring he would be adopted and gone so would save me from having to disappoint the girls. I wanted to move on to finding a "real dog."

They finally badgered me enough I made the darn call. And guess what? He was still available. And they really needed to get him out of there, they needed room and he had been there too long. "Yay," I thought with the least enthusiasm I could muster.

Now the rescue was pressuring me to come adopt that dog. Fine. I'm stuck. I'll get the stupid dog for my girls.

I went to the rescue and started the process of taking the dog home. Straight to the office for paperwork I went. I had to sign off on a bunch of things I never did nor would do, got the rundown on the dog: two to three years old, came from kill shelter where he was about to be put down, very shy and loves his tummy rubbed ("he'll roll over every time we get near to have his tummy rubbed"), blah blah blah, and "that'll be $117."

"$117!? Whatthe? That's twice as much as I expected." Ugh.

So all done with formalities, she goes back to bring me "my new family member." The instant she walks back through the door, all I can think is, "Is that the right dog?"

"It sure is," I am informed.

"Did he shrink?"

"Hahaha nnnnooooo. Here."

And away I went. It's no more than ten miles from the rescue to my house and that dog fell asleep less than half way home. I was convinced they drugged that dog to make him appear calm and relaxed. Come to find out no they did not; if that dog wasn't sleeping, he was yawning. He was naturally relaxed. Also turns out it's not that he likes his belly rubbed so rolls over when approached, he was severely abused and petrified to be approached so was cowering. His tail was broken and never fixed so had a crook in it. His face was already starting to gray so he was not two or three. Nor four or five. I thought more like six to eight and the vet confirmed that yes, he was about seven or eight. What in the world had I gotten myself into?

Turns out he was a Chiweenie–a Chihuahua / Dachshund mix. This dog was as close to a cat as you could come and still be a canine.

Ooohhh but the girls adored him. They named him Donner which means thunder and strong. They wanted him to have a strong, bold name so he didn't realize how small and cowardly he was. They adored him, so wanted to be with him all the time. I wanted to keep close tabs on him from the beginning so I could make sure he was behaving himself.

And behave himself he did. He never barked. Ever. After a few months my boyfriend taught him how to bark. He thought it was "fun" to do that. He had a few little accidents but only when I left him alone for long work shifts. He didn't chew anything. This dog was obviously severely beaten but didn't have any bad habits or behaviors so I don't know why. He must have been beaten out of pure cruelty.

We've had Donner over four years now. He doesn't cower whenever you put your shoes on or pick up the broom much anymore, he plays with toys, he doesn't bark unnecessarily, and I'm pretty sure he smiles sometimes. It is such a pleasure to have a dog that seems to really appreciate being part of a home and being loved. The girls still love him.

As for me and my feelings about him: I'm not positive when it all turned around but he's my doggie and I love him. I adore him. He still greets me like a cat would, pretty nonchalantly, but I know he loves me too. He hasn't picked up any bad habits, he's quiet, cute and even sleeps with me. He is my best little buddy and I can't imagine him not being a part of our little family.

***

Jesse the Dog

By Anne Post

I wanted a dog when I was growing up in suburban Baltimore, but my parents would only allow a cat. Flea was a cool cat, but no replacement for a dog.

As soon as I was on my own living in southern Idaho, I thought about owning a dog. I worked for Idaho Fish and Game on a project that required flushing pheasants to count them. A good friend told me that a couple in her home town of St. Mary's had a litter of Springer Spaniel pups. Springers are bird hunting dogs who flush instead of pointing, just the kind of dog I needed. She was a registered Springer from hunting stock, not show stock, smaller with shorter fur the better to get through the brush and brambles to flush hidden birds. The family next door to my childhood home had one and I was excited at the possibility of finally owning one.

I had never chosen a puppy before, but was told to look for a pup who was independent. A little female ventured further than the others and went off exploring the yard on her own.

I named her Palouse Jesse after the wheat fields of the Palouse region in Northern Idaho where she was born and I was attending school. She turned out to be kindest, sweetest dog, totally devoted to me.

I made mistakes raising her even though I had a lot of help from co-workers who trained hunting dogs. I was asked to babysit five little kids at one time and brought her along. They were all shrieking and running around and playing with the young pup and I thought that she was having a great time. Didn't realize that she was scared and overstimulated. From that day on she didn't like kids. When I lived across the street from an elementary school, if unsuspecting children walked by she would charge off the porch and chase them all the way to school.

We had more than a few adventures together. At Fish and Game we drove clunky old pickup trucks and the dogs would ride on top of the utility box in the open bed. I came off an exit ramp and kept driving until we reached the plot we were going to survey. I hopped out of the truck and there was no pup in the back!

She had fallen out somewhere along the route. We drove back the way we had come, with me getting more panicked with every passing mile. I fully expected to see my dog dead on the road, or thought someone had picked her up and I would never see her again. We finally drove past the exit ramp and she was lying next to a light pole, where she probably slid off.

Instead of running off to find me she waited for me to come back, never doubting that I would. Thankfully she wasn't injured. I covered the box with carpet so it wasn't so slippery, but she rode in the cab with me until she got older and learned to hang on.

When she was a small pup, I was afraid someone would steal her as there was a market for purebred hunting dogs in Southern Idaho. I kept a watchful eye but she managed to elude me a couple of times.

Once I went in the front door of a store, came out and she was missing. I was scared to death that she was abducted, but finally went around to the back of the store and there she was waiting for me. I never understood why she thought I would go in the front and come out the back but she wasn't taking any chances I would get away. She was always thinking and I had to try to outsmart her.

She remained that way her whole life—always wanting to be with me. When we moved to Juneau my boyfriend (soon to be husband) and I shared one little yellow Toyota pickup truck. I dropped him off at work each day and Jesse the dog made several trips with us from our little house in the Mendenhall Valley to the U.S. Forest Service office a few miles away. One day I came home from work and the dog was missing! I searched all over the neighborhood and couldn't find her. I was frantic when my boyfriend came home and said someone at the Forest Service office had seen a little brown and white Springer Spaniel hanging around. She finally made it home later that evening. We figured she had decided to find me and remembered the route to the Forest Service office which crossed several busy roads and a four-lane highway. We couldn't believe she remembered the way just from riding in a truck, and made it there and back safely!

Jesse and I did a road trip from Idaho to the East Coast. My college housemate came along as far as Ohio. His parents' fancy home had expensive white carpets throughout, so I pitched a small tent and slept in their perfectly manicured back yard. His mother was mortified and apologetic, but Jesse and I were totally comfortable.

She gave birth to three beautiful puppies—a very unplanned event. Initially I didn't even realize she was pregnant. After the first pup was born she hopped up on my bed at 2 a.m. and woke me up. I was so touched that she wanted to share the experience of giving birth with me. I always wished she could have been there for the birth of my babies.

But she died just after I got married on the East Coast. Our house sitter wasn't familiar with dogs and left a bag of chocolate chips on the kitchen table. Jessy ate most of it and threw up. She locked the dog in the windowless garage and left the garage door up just a few inches. Jesse had never been kept there and she was desperate to get out. She chewed the rubber gasket off the bottom of the door and swallowed some pieces. She died of gastric torsion, a condition when the stomach flips over–a painful way to go.

Her suffering and death broke my heart into a million pieces. I've never been so devastated; I've never had such unconditional love. She just wanted to be by my side and please me. I mourned her death more than my mother's. Looking down at my mother in her coffin, I felt sad, but nothing like the heartbreak of unexpectedly losing my dog–a dog that had been by my side for seven years through a series of romantic relationships, graduate school stress and a move to Alaska.

I wrote the breeders, telling them how much she had enriched my life and asking if they had more puppies. They had stopped breeding dogs, sent regrets, and thanked me for providing such a good life for her. And they included a copy of her official pedigree record listing her mother and father as still alive, but her as dead. In black and white it hit me so hard that I had to stop and catch my breath. There would never be another dog like her ever again.

To my surprise, there was. A Border Collie Labrador mix pup that we found in Juneau when my kids were in middle school. I took them out of school to look at the litter a few weeks before they were ready to leave their mother. She was the runt with jet black fur and piercing ice blue eyes the color of the Mendenhall Glacier. My husband named her Lazer Beam. She followed us to the end of the driveway that day and sat there watching us drive away. She chose us. Smartest dog we have ever owned and also totally devoted to us. She passed away four years ago and this time the whole family had our hearts broken.

Since Lazer died I had been looking all over the country for another Border Collie Labrador mix. Amazingly we found a pup right here in Juneau and we started our saga anew. It's too early to tell what kind of dog Isabelle (Izzy) will turn out to be, but like the others she's very smart and keeps us on our toes, constantly trying to outthink us.

As for Jesse the Dog—we call her that to distinguish her from Jessy our daughter—I still have her ashes. Someday I will hike up Mt. McGinnis, her last hike with me, and deposit some there. And I'll scatter some in my garden at my house in Juneau that overlooks the ocean, where I plan to have my ashes scattered too.

Chapter Twenty-One

Maybe it's not so much about social media as it is about those who partake in it, and how they do so. Perhaps the challenge of effective communication, and how it presents itself in the digital era, really isn't that much different than our bygone past after all.

Allan Besselink

Digital Friendship

Do electronic media unite us or divide us? Yes and yes.

KELLEN & FRIENDS

Fantasy Football. Look around at real-life players from throughout the National Football League, pick your favorites and form an imaginary team of your own creation.

Then on Sunday football afternoons set out beer, pizza, chips and salsa and gather to watch and cheer your chosen players in real time. Rack up points through your players' catches, interceptions, touch-downs.

Fantasy Football is the tie that binds these high school classmates.

They graduated from 1999 through 2001, and began Fantasy Football in 2002 with a group of eight. Four of the original members are still playing; the same group playing today has been together since 2007.

Most of the current group of 10 have known each other since elementary school; one of the 10 is Kellen Wefing's dad, Kim. Seven still live in the same rural area in Western New York, one lives in Lakewood, Ohio, one in Columbus, Ohio, one in Washington, D.C.

They come by their interest naturally. Nine of the 10 played football in high school, including Kellen's father. Two of them, brothers, played college football, at Alfred University and at University of Buffalo.

The one-time classmates work in sales, as high school teachers, chef, general manager, FBI agent, UPS driver.

In August, before the NFL season starts, players from Ohio drive back home to New York, the one living in Washington turns to Skype and all 10 gather in Kim's garage to draft their own teams.

Game days, Sundays during the football season, each team is matched against another in the group. They can also trade players, just like real NFL managers. It is a sport made possible by technology. A program through Yahoo records and calculates points, and keeps a history of participants that Kellen could trace back to their 2002 beginnings.

Just to make it more interesting, each participant throws in $150. Top six teams go into playoffs. Winner takes home $800, second place, $400. Third gets his $150 back.

While fantasy football is the glue, it is not the totality of their relationship. All but Kellen and one other are married; he has been in five of their weddings. They have 11 children among them. But through the football season long time friends make time for each other.

In summer Kellen plays golf with three of them.

But he acknowledges that without the bond of Fantasy Football it is less likely they would stay in touch.

***

Friendship Beyond Facebook

Robin is a teenager living in Kürten, Germany. You can find him on Facebook, under an abbreviated name, mostly on pages of other people. But he doesn't dwell there.

"What if you have 1,000 'friends' on Facebook but you are sitting home alone?!" he asks. "The intensity of the word 'friend/you are my friend' has changed.

"You can only be close to somebody in real life. In a close relationship you can't feign your feelings. But in social media there are a lot of living people. That is one of the reasons I stopped using social media like Facebook, Instagram or Snapchat.

"For some people it is really difficult to find very good friends and have close relationships with them. Because they feel like nobody is listening to them, they always listen to others and give them advice for their problems. That is because human beings are egoists. At first you have to look into yourself and ask: have I ever mentioned my problems to my friends? If yes and your friends did not care, they aren't good friends at all.

"Good friends are those who listen to you. Who share their problems and experiences with you. A good friendship is based/founded on giving and taking. You laugh, you cry, and you feel with your friends. You and your friend are often having the same thoughts.

"A friend is somebody you identify with. It doesn't matter where they are from. Friendship has no borders. I mean no physical borders (like country borders) and no mental borders. Even age is no border between friends.

"I for myself have some older friends. I like to listen to their stories and experiences. And I learned a lot from them, that I shared with my same age friends."

Chapter Twenty-Two

What is the secret of a strong joyous life?
Hugh Black

I had a friend.
Charles Kingsley

The Serious Side of Friendship

He lived through the life-altering 1992 Hurricane Andrew, which ripped and scattered homes and severed power lines like pieces of string. In the difficult days that followed he and others were buoyed by the kindness of strangers bringing food, water and comfort. The hurricane forged a deep sense of community among survivors. As normal life slowly resumed, so did the distances. People went back to work, to school, to their homes, and they grew apart again.

HEALTH FOR BODY AND PSYCHE

Vice Admiral Vivek Murthy, U.S. Surgeon General 2014-2017, personally experienced how tragedy brings people together, and how fleeting that connection is.

As Surgeon General he witnessed how loneliness affected people of every age and socioeconomic background. As a practicing physician the most common pathology he saw was not heart disease or diabetes. It was loneliness.

He calls loneliness a growing health epidemic. Despite being connected by technology in ways unimaginable in the 1990s, rates of people who say they are lonely have doubled since then. Further, their health is at risk. While studies are rife and often questionable, one claims that loneliness and weak social connections may reduce life span as much as smoking 15 cigarettes a day.

Most of the friendships in this book were forged predigital era. For all our online connectedness, more people feel isolated today. We are inherently social beings. It will be the task of today's generation to find meaningful ways to connect within this new framework.

Frequent moves, often for employment of a family member, provide another barrier to forming long-term friendships. One child of a military father who moved to a new school almost every year developed a stage persona with bright smile and outgoing personality that masked who she truly was. It is a facade she still cannot break through decades later.

At the Green Arch diner in Brocton, NY, friends gathered every morning to discuss daily events. Most were regulars, meeting every day, sitting around the same table in the same chair. It is like that across America and perhaps the world. Diners, coffee shops, restaurants where people gather, and talk and coffee flows.

Benefits of coffee are indisputable.

Longer life with reduced risks of colorectal cancer and liver diseases, even while drinking up to eight cups a day. Increased metabolism, speeding bodily functions and assisting in fat burning and weight loss. Lower risk of weight-related problems, such as type 2 diabetes. All according to studies from august medical organizations like the American Medical Association and Harvard School of Public Health.

Lower risk and perhaps even prevention of Alzheimer's and Parkinson's diseases, and dementia, says Harvard School of Public Health.

Coffee improves memory, mood, vigilance, energy levels, reaction times and general cognitive function, controlled trials showed. No surprise to drivers trying to stay awake alone on the road at night, students pulling all-nighters during finals week, and writers who make coffee a steady companion in their solitary occupation.

Most Americans get more antioxidants from coffee than from fruits and vegetables combined, a benefit that may decrease risk of heart disease and stroke.

Pretty heavy lifting for a beverage many of us would drink anyhow, in the amount of about 400 million cups a day in the United States, 4 billion cups world-wide.

But it's also a beverage to be shared, on its own in coffee shops or after a meal with family and friends.

Some of the diseases born of loneliness are the same ones that coffee may prevent. Perhaps it is not just the coffee after all, but the human relationships it fosters.

Is it caffeine, companionship or some combination of both?

After moving from my former home town, one of the things I missed most was meeting Kathy for coffee. It wasn't the coffee and rolls that mattered most, nor the uncommon view of mountains. It was the sharing of our lives. Mountain vistas aside, it wasn't so different from what happened at the Brocton Diner and countless other places around the world. Caffeine plus companionship may make our lives longer, they surely make our lives better.

Brad Jarrett, a fitness professional in Jamestown, NY, wrote a column in the *Chautauqua Star* entitled "The One Thing You Need to be Heathy." Exercise and healthy eating matter, he said, but "I firmly believe relationships are more important than any 'exercise' in the gym."

It is hard to imagine a life without friends. Yet there are people who say they do not have any. How often, when we hear of acts of violence, do neighbors say the perpetrator was quiet and kept to himself? That they never saw any friends come to the house. "A loner who never had friends visit or call," a former supervisor said of a man who mailed more than a dozen bombs to prominent politicians with whom he disagreed. Friendship not only enriches us, it can save us and keep us human.

Can people learn how to make friends? A plethora of books and blogs declare it is so. Dale Carnegie's immensely popular, enduring *How to Win Friends and Influence People*, was published in 1937, sold 15 million copies and is still being reprinted. Geared in part to winning financial success, his rules for making friends include genuine interest in other people, appreciating them and their point of view, letting them know you care about them.

Two earlier classic works on friendship were written by men for men, as though women didn't have or need consequential friendships, or perhaps didn't need their advice. Both inhabited a time when men and women lived in different spheres with unequal education and work opportunities. Both have a strong emphasis on theology, Scripture and that extra component in friendship they refer to as the soul.

In *The Four Loves,* C.S. Lewis says friendship arises out of a common interest or insight but includes something more. That "something more" is a kindred soul. Friends will do things together, but also share something more inward.

"People who simply 'want friends' can never make any," he asserts. Friendship requires a shared vision, the same truth; without that friendship cannot arise.

"Friendship must be about something."

Lewis, a prolific author born in Belfast, Ireland in 1898, also contended something that may not ring as true today—that we do not want to know our friend's affairs. That we initially become friends without knowing if the other is single or married or how they make a living.

That is beside the point, he felt.

"The real question: 'Do you see the same truth?' In a circle of two Friends (he always capitalizes 'Friends') each man is simply what he is: stands for nothing but himself."

Protestant theologian Hugh Black's book, *Friendship,* was published in 1898 when he was just 30 years old. Born in Scotland in1868, he immigrated to the United States in 1906 to accept a position at Union Theological Seminary in New York City.

"There can never be true friendship without self-respect, and unless soul meets soul free from self-seeking," Black wrote.

Believe that you are a person of worth. Set your ego aside. Care as much for the success of others as for your own.

"There is nothing so important as the choice of friendship; for it both reflects character and affects it," he said.

"There can only be friendship between equals—not necessarily in social position or intellectual attainment, but equality that has a spiritual source."

Moving past the more florid language of their days, both Black and Lewis speak to our universal need for a meaningful connection with others.

"The perfect friendship is grounded on what is permanent, on goodness, on character. It is of much slower growth, since it takes time to really find out the truly lovable things in a life, but it is lasting, since the foundation is stable," Black wrote.

One of the gifts that comes with years is learning which friendships endure, transcending time and distance.

"True friendship is a plant of slow growth," George Washington wrote to his favorite nephew, Bushrod Washington, who was in law school. The letter dated January 15, 1783, was full of advice about distinguishing himself in his chosen profession, choosing friends thoughtfully, dressing conservatively, avoiding gaming.

"Be courteous to all but intimate with few, and let those few be well tried before you give them your confidence; true friendship is a plant of slow growth, and must undergo and withstand the shocks of adversity before it is entitled to appellation."

Hubert H. Humphrey, U.S. Senator, vice-president, presidential candidate, college professor, husband and father of four, said "the greatest gift of life is friendship, and I have received it." Not political power with its trappings, not even family. Friendship. Indeed various studies indicated that friends are more important than family in longevity and a sense of well-being.

Rebecca Adams, professor of sociology at University of North Carolina, says the definition of friendship depends on who you ask. It may vary by ethnicity, economic class, age or

gender. Men tend to mention doing things with their friends, and women remark about sharing intimacies with theirs.

She says that the role of friendship in our lives generally isn't very well appreciated. "There is just scads of stuff on families and marriage, but very little on friendship. It baffles me."

A decade after Alaska passed from Russian to U.S. hands, S. Hall Young arrived in 1878 to become Presbyterian missionary to the Tlingit Indians. The following summer a boat steamed into his Wrangell parish bearing three senior officials of his church and their wives with money and plans for his mission work. But more significant personally, as he wrote in his autobiography, "the greatest event of the summer and, indeed, of my life in Alaska, was the arrival on the same steamer of a fourth big man—America's greatest naturalist—John Muir.

"I know that there was an intangible but very real bond of union between Muir and me from the time our hands first met in that clasp of friendship; the strongest and warmest friendship I have ever experienced in a life blessed with many friends."

"I believe friendship is the most genuinely humane relationship of which we are capable," Daisaku Ikeda, Buddhist philosopher and founding president of the Soka Gakkai International, wrote. "To be understood and appreciated for oneself is a vital experience in life, strengthening our will to live in seen and unseen ways.

"From my experience, friendship is not a matter of the amount of time you spend with someone. Rather, it is a measure of the strength and depth of the spiritual resonance that arises between you. Many times, meeting someone for the first time, I have felt an indescribable sense of familiarity."

A friend gave my soon-to-be husband and me a copy of *The Prophet* in the late 1960s, when the Kahlil Gibran classic was selling 240,000 copies a year. When I went to a garage sale recently and saw a copy on the shelf, the owner was almost apologetic, quick to explain she bought it to write a wedding toast years ago and hadn't looked at it since. Not so much in vogue now, it has never been out of print and has been published in 40 languages.

I have read and re-read *The Prophet,* even using excerpts on home-made greeting cards. From his essay on friendship: "Your friend is your needs answered...And he is your board and your fireside.

"If a friend is there to buoy you up in times of need, also share in times of joy."

And my favorite, "let there be no purpose in friendship save the deepening of the spirit."

Gibran, a philosopher who blended Christianity, Islam and the Baha'i faith and said the whole earth is his homeland, is a voice for today.

Even the United Nations recognized the power of friendship. It has proclaimed a profusion of days worthy of remembrance, weighty subjects like social justice and zero discrimination. But perhaps none more universal than International Day of Friendship.

It officially recognized July 30th as International Friendship Day in 2011, although most countries celebrate it on the first Sunday of August.

Ban Ki-moon, U.N. Secretary General at the time, wrote "Friendship is a joy in itself, conferring happiness and a sense of wellbeing. And the accumulation of bonds of camaraderie around the world can contribute to fundamental shifts that are urgently needed to achieve lasting stability.

"The forces of division that actively try to undermine peace, security and social harmony are no match for the simple but powerful act of extending a hand in our own personal circles and especially beyond. Ties of trust can weave a safety net that will protect us all. As understanding and awareness grow, we can build compassion and generate passion for a better world where all are united for the greater good."

Could friendships not only save us, but save the world?

Friendship grows softly over time, with shared conversations, phone calls, texts, a cup of coffee, a glass of wine. As gradually as it started, it may taper off with scarcely a notice. One day they are gone from our life. We don't even notice until they flicker across our mind and we wonder "whatever happened to her?"

Why? Why do some leave and some stay, as steadfast as winter turns to spring? Sometimes we no longer work at the same place. We no longer live in the same town. One marries or has a baby or gets a divorce. Sometimes a misunderstanding spans too many years and cannot be bridged. Sometimes we reconnect. Sometimes, through it all, friendship remains intact.

The miracle is those relationships that span time and distance and changing stations in life, and remain fast.

ABOUT THE AUTHOR

Judy Shuler lives near Lake Erie in rural Western New York.

Contact the author at enduringfriendship.com

www.ingramcontent.com/pod-product-compliance
Lightning Source LLC
Chambersburg PA
CBHW071349290426
44108CB00014B/1484